# Let's Start a Riot

# Let's Start a Riot

## How a Young Drunk Punk Became a Hollywood Dad

### Bruce McCulloch

HarperCollins*Publishers*Ltd

Published by HarperCollins Publishers Ltd

First Canadian edition

Interior photos appear courtesy of the author.

HarperCollins books may be purchased for educational, business,
or sales promotional use through our Special Markets Department.

HarperCollins Publishers Ltd
2 Bloor Street East, 20th Floor
Toronto, Ontario, Canada
M4W 1A8

*www.harpercollins.ca*

Library and Archives Canada Cataloguing in Publication
information is available upon request

ISBN 978-1-44342-638-1

Printed and bound in the United States of America
RRD 9 8 7 6 5 4 3 2 1

*This book is dedicated to all the furniture at the side of the road.*
*And all the people who have left it there.*
*And the other people who pick it up and take it home.*

Some of the names have been altered to protect the innocent.

For me, there is no hiding . . .

# Contents

# Let's Start a Riot

# I Love Bruce

Winter 1991. Toronto, Ontario. The streets of the Canadian megacity are covered with snow. My then-girlfriend/now-wife, Laurie, was the manager of Brian Hartt, one of the writers on *The Kids in the Hall*, and we are there to visit him. Earlier in the day, we've gone to the set and watched the Kids film part of a sketch. I've glimpsed Bruce from afar. I am an enormous Kids in the Hall fan and an especially rabid fan of Bruce's, whose characters and performance style I have always marvelled at. He has a delivery unlike anyone I have ever seen in comedy before, and I am desperate to meet him.

That night, we meet up with the Kids at a bar and I am able to nervously have a conversation with Bruce for a good ten minutes. He is pleasant but aloof, distracted by both people he knows and by adoring fans. But we have a good talk, and even though its content is lost in the nervous haze I get into whenever I find myself face to face with one of my heroes, I leave the conversation feeling like Bruce and I have made a nice connection.

The next night, Brian tells us he's meeting Bruce at a different bar and asks if we would like to come. This is my chance to cement my friendship with Bruce. We arrive at the bar, and I sit at a table where Bruce is holding court. He looks at me and I say with great familiarity, "Hey, Bruce, I'm Paul. We hung out last night."

Upon which Bruce looks at me icily for several seconds and then says, "No, we didn't hang out. We talked."

And then he goes back to conversing with the other people at the table and never looks at me again.

And that was the beginning of my long and wonderful friendship with Bruce McCulloch.

I don't remember when we actually became friends, or even why. Our paths crossed again because of Brian, and suddenly, we hit it off. It was like that moment when the big, scary dog in the neighbourhood that always chased you and wanted to kill you comes up tentatively and lets you pet him.

I haven't technically petted Bruce, but I did marry him to his lovely wife. I've holed up with him in his former house in Toronto to write, and we both drank so much Jim Beam and Coke that after a week neither of us could fit into our pants. He got me into collecting Canadian art. He turned me on to some of my favourite alternative bands. He taught me the joys of peeing off the stoop in your backyard instead of using the indoor toilet.

We've been through several dogs together, supported each other through our various movie and TV projects, and had some of the greatest discussions about comedy, writing, directing and life in general that I've ever been involved in.

Simply put, I love Bruce.

As I alluded to earlier, Bruce is truly unique. When we say in comedy that somebody has "a voice," Bruce is the very definition of what we're talking about. His take on the world, his characters, his writing, his one-man shows, the actual *voice* that comes out of his mouth—they're all unique.

When I sat in his Toronto kitchen in the mid-1990s and he informally read me his one-man show, *Slightly Bigger Cities*, I was blown away. He had me laughing, he choked me up, he made me think. I had done stand-up comedy for years but never could have conceived of communicating to an audience in that way. He's both a reliable and unreliable narrator, a spinner of tales tall and real, a bobbing-and-weaving wordsmith who makes you burst out laughing a moment before he hits you with some truth that stops you in your tracks.

But most of all, he's funny.

So sit back, lick your thumb to turn the pages (even if you're using an e-reader) and enjoy the voice and world of my good friend—a man whom I don't hang out with but simply talk to—the amazing Bruce McCulloch.

—Paul Feig

# Let's Start a Riot

I am a writer. A simple man pushing and pulling words around. My whole life, I have been asking myself, "What are you thinking? . . . Hey, do you have an idea?" Stopping conversations in the middle to write down a phrase. I have a series of tartan notebooks that I have been scrawling in since I was a teenager. Perhaps I carried these around to tell myself, and the world, that I was a writer. These books became coffee- and time-stained as I toted them from place to place. My own illegible library.

Inside of me, there has always been the arrogant dream of writing a book. One day. When I was old. Luckily, and unluckily, that day had come. I had just gotten off the phone with my

Busy Agent. I was excited by the news that I was going to be writing a book. I wanted to tell someone. But who? No friends came to mind. I couldn't really tell the gardeners, could I? I didn't know the Spanish word for "book." (I later looked it up. It's *el libro,* in case you ever need to know it.) Also, the gardeners can be kind of cold, like they're mad at me or something. Maybe I'm just being paranoid. Then it hit me: of course! If I have good news, I should tell my family. My Pretty Wife and two kids who allow me to live in their house. That I pay for. Somehow.

They burst through the door. Roscoe and Heidi. They're five and seven, I think. I don't remember and they won't tell me. And it seems that as soon as I remember their ages, *poof,* one of them has a birthday.

Heidi is seven, and a big seven. She's nine hands high. She can eat six oranges in one sitting. She can jump over a bouncy castle in a single leap. But while she's big for her age, she is still a baby at heart.

Roscoe, on the other hand, is an ad for a boy. A dancing, gentle, happy but not stupid boy. A smallish five, but still he knows how to toddle over and refresh your wine glass. He knows which wine you were—or should be—drinking. In fact, his first word was "Malbec." And he pours with compassion. He knows what you've been through. He knows what you're going through. He's on track to become a teenage sommelier. Yes, we recently enrolled him in a course they offer at school for kids with "gifted palates." There was a waiting list, but I got him bumped up. That's the extent of my power in Hollywood. *That* and the fact that I can leave a message for anyone in town.

Roscoe is crying. Already crying, or still crying, I wonder. He is hard to understand at the best of times, but when he's blubbering, all bets are off. His older sister translates. Something to do with him getting a yellow belt in karate but not getting a yellow belt in karate?

"Well, Daddy's got some interesting news too."

Heidi responds, "Apple in a bowl." Meaning, "Asshole, go get me my apple cut up in a bowl like you do every day at this time." My daughter has blood-sugar issues. At least we hope that's what it is. Got it. Apple cut up perfectly in the correctly coloured bowl, then my news.

"Roscoe, what do you want to eat?" He looks at me and cries a jazzy wallow.

"Butter sandwich with fish crackers inside," says Heidi.

He cries another good blast. "With the crusts cut off. You can eat the crusts, Daddy." In this house, Daddy gets the crusts. I am a crust eater. I am an apple butler. I am Daddy.

Heidi is old for her age, but I'm sure she wouldn't think so. One day when she was five, I came home and she said, "Hey, where's my sushi?"

"I didn't know you liked sushi. How would I know you liked sushi?"

"Didn't you get my text?"

"I didn't know you knew how to text."

Now she is going through a phase (at least we hope it's a phase): she's been wearing glasses that she doesn't need. Prop glasses with lenses, but she is very serious about them. She is so cute in the morning when she wakes up, lurches out and fumbles for them as if she can't possibly see without them. When she puts them on and yawns, I can imagine her being an old woman someday.

Enter, my Pretty Wife, carrying an armful of catalogues from the mailbox that sits atop our driveway. They just keep inventing new things for her to need. The catalogue people have her in their sights. Consumerism disguised as creativity. She's also carrying fresh locally sourced organic foods from the farmer's market. Or "overpriced" as I often (always) refer to them. But more pressingly, she has two almost identical tile samples for the kitchen floor that I only realized needed replacing when I was told it needed replacing. She has to decide and call her Tile Guy right away. He is a very busy, in-demand Tile Guy. She has a Cheese Guy, a Fish Guy, a Condiments Man and, now, a Tile Guy. I get the quick image of some lunk with calloused hands, not computer-soft like mine, pulling down her Lululemon yoga pants to get at her MILFy goods. But I stop myself because I have good news to tell her.

I want to say, "Actually, I'm going to be working on a book that will pay for part of that floor." But she's engrossed in studying these samples in natural light. And by the way, isn't all light natural? Roscoe has forgotten karate and is now dancing. Our little Lord of the Dance is suddenly quite happy. He's dancing on each sample to see which is "faster." My Pretty Wife calls her sister to get her opinion of the tiles over the phone. She describes them both, and refers to the one that she's now leaning towards as "well worth the money."

Heidi is not impressed. Which is common. She grabs the prop glasses that sit on a chain around her neck, puts them on and rolls her eyes. She goes back to her own project: picking out books from a catalogue she's been given at school. Which five should she get? For sure for sure, she wants the one about a girl whose sister is a vampire. Or she's a vampire, I wasn't really listening. But I thought, "Duh, book? I'm going tell her I'm writing a book." Life has given me a natural segue. That never happens! (Sorry about the exclamation mark. I'll try not to do that again.)

Those of you blessed and/or cursed with a family know that a family is a big, lurching boat. You try to stay upright while doing your job. Only every so often do you lock eyes with one of the shipmates who make up your family. Mostly, you are busy. And alone. It's loud but lonely. Sometimes beautiful things, or moments, fly by you and you miss them. Or you notice them and promise yourself to be touched by them later.

After a few minutes, I sit slumped by the fire. My Pretty Wife brings me the martini I ordered some time ago. But in all fairness, the kitchen has been backed up with kids' complicated dinner orders. She joins me. Our first moment together all day. She smiles. So loving and calm for an instant. The girl I married. She asks me about my day. Did anything interesting happen? I look at her, but for some reason I . . . don't want to tell her about the book. I am now like a baby-man in a snit of my own creation. I can't get my good mood back, no matter how hard I try. Even though I'm not really trying. Finally, I make her pull it out of me. She is ecstatic.

I act distracted and even lob, "Let's talk about the tile some more. Aren't there other people you could phone to help you decide?" She doesn't bite. She calls the kids in and tells them, "Daddy is going to write a book." Roscoe is elated, but doesn't seem to know what a book is. Though he immediately knows it should be called *Let's Start a Riot*. As if to lobby for his idea, he starts to run around in riotous circles. It is very loud and annoying, but at least he's getting exercise. *Let's Start a Riot*? Daddy's the writer here; I think he can come up with a better title than that.

"Really? Like what?" asks my Pretty Wife, suddenly not so pretty.

"I've got a few I'm rolling around in my head. Nothing I'm quite ready to pitch."

Heidi, as always, is worried.

She says, "A book will be a lot of work for you. Are you sure you can do it?"

"Of course I can do it," I say.

"What will this book be about?" she asks.

Everything stops. All eyes on me. The house is quiet for the first time in weeks.

"Well," I stammer, "it'll be about how I was once a young, angry punk who crawled out of a crappy family, had this silly show on TV, then somehow became a happy man, with a pretty good family." Crickets.

"Why would anyone want to read that?" Heidi asks.

"People like Daddy," offers my wife. "Those who know him."

Gee, thanks. I feel clammy. I try to remember what I had said in the meeting.

"People will enjoy my book because it will be funny and touching and sort of relatable."

Heidi just glares. My wife freezes a smile on her face. Avoidingly, I grab my laptop to check to see if there were any emails since the last time I checked to see if there were any emails.

Heidi prods, "Are you writing the book now?"

"No."

"You better start. I'm getting worried."

"Get off my back. I'll start first thing in the morning."

"Don't you usually watch TV first thing in the morning?"

"Heidi, sometimes Daddy catches up with what is going on in the world in the morning."

"You do that by watching *House Hunters International*?"

"What are you, a tiny cop?"

She moves towards the kitchen, then stops. She gets serious. "Dad, your book sounds sort of boring. I think you have to put a vampire in it." I finish my martini and think to myself, "Oh, I will. You and Roscoe and Mom are all vampires." There will be others, of course.

In the kitchen, my Pretty Wife knowingly begins to rattle the martini shaker. We both know I have some work to do . . .

# *Hollywood*

I live in the Hollywood Hills with my two kids and my Pretty Wife. She's a good Canadian girl. Wonderful lady. She answers every question before it's even asked. Catches every tear, real or imagined, before it hits the carpet. She's tough as nails, but whenever she finishes a book, she cries, knowing she'll miss all her "friends" inside those pages. She can organize a Moms Club fundraiser in her sleep. She actually did just that. I heard her somnambulistically mumbling details.

And, most impressively, she played Nancy Drew in a short-lived series in the '90s. I take great pleasure in that fact. So whenever she loses her car keys, I can say, "Why can't you find them? Aren't you Nancy Drew?!" I've even got the kids doing it: "Mom, why can't you find my glow-in-the-dark shoes? I thought you were Nancy Drew!"

Also, as we were getting married, and she was coming up the aisle towards me, I could have sworn I heard her mutter under her breath, "I love it when a plan comes together." Perhaps I'm being paranoid.

We are now an old couple. You know you are an old couple when you can share the same eyeglasses. We have been married a long time, but still every so often she gives me "the look." The look I know so well. The look that says, "Let's just stay in tonight and get wasted and watch *Intervention*." We watch that show because it puts our drinking in perspective. Sure, we like a drink now and then, but we're not like *those* people!

Sometimes, people compare marriage to a war. I don't think that is fair at all. Because in a war, if you surrender, you get to stop.

I am a writer with a complicated career. Meaning sometimes I work, sometimes I don't. It's gloomy when I don't work. It can be stormy when I do. Married to a writer, my wife must endure and hope. But *I* have to do the writing. So we both have our crosses to bear.

So here I sit in Hollywood, part success story, part caution-ary tale. Successful because I tend to sell things—movie scripts, TV pilots, etc. But cautionary because they mostly don't "go." Meaning, get made. I have realized no one ever stops you on the street to quote from these scripts. Or reads them aloud at your funeral. Or perhaps even goes to your funeral.

I live in a bubble house. A starter mansion, as I quip. But honestly, I try not to quip. Perhaps I *should* quip and my scripts would get made more often. I can't see the Hollywood sign from where I am, but they assure me it's there. Lurking. Waiting to inspire or taunt. Some days, I ask my housekeeper, Nadia, if, on her way into work, she can check to see if it's still standing. It's one of the jokes that we enjoy. That she doesn't understand.

It's a bubble house. When I bought it, it was a perfect time to buy. But in truth, it wasn't. Where is my breathless real estate agent now? Now is not a perfect time to sell. I'm like all the hopeful fools who wanted to get "in" before it was too late. I got in, and now it's too late. When I first took possession, as I walked up the cracked driveway, I could have sworn that I heard "I Gotcha" by Joe Tex playing. Now I'm underwater. I swim around the place, seemingly in slow motion. Underwater. Treading water. I mutter to myself, "Don't blame the house."

But secretly, I do. It sucked me in with its mid-century noncha-lance. Now I'm trapped here.

I empty the dishwasher. Then float around, turning off lights that are always left on. By the time I get back to the dishwasher, it needs emptying again. Somehow. It's an endless Sisyphean loop that I call my life.

Now, when I dream, I no longer dream of riches or redheads. I dream of having that guy from *Income Property* come take care of me. You know that show? Its host, a handsome man with flowing, if complicated, hair and beautiful two-storey teeth, finds people and helps them renovate income suites cheaply and cheerfully. Down to the studs, and he certainly is one.

I dream he comes to meet me as my family and I arrive at the Toronto airport. He promises to find us a house with rental potential so the cheques can "start rolling into the bank." Soon, I am hanging on his every word. But truthfully, it is *him* I want to hang on to.

He and I would house-hunt with manly vigour. Stopping for the occasional Double Double at Tim Hortons. We'd stir our coffee and laugh. He's so tough, he'd actually stir his with his index finger. I'd tell him about my life. He'd tell me about government-approved fire doors. Under his strong, but kind tutelage, I would buy a house. Under asking. Or perhaps he would hold my hand through a rapacious bidding war. Either way, I would win. *We* would win.

Days later, he would open his laptop and give me two options. Option one: a full gut job. And option two: a full gut job—that he and I would do behind my wife's back. I take option two.

Together, we would demolish. His muscles bulging. My muscles just watching. The soaring sound of Skilsaws would soon segue to the soundtrack of us working and laughing.

One day, as the sawdust cleared, our eyes would lock. He'd float towards me and try to kiss me. We'd bump our protective glasses and giggle. I'd look at him. "But I'm not gay." He'd say, "I'm not gay, either, but I think the house is. Things are uncovered when you peel back the walls."

The day of the reveal, he'd wear tight pants, I'd wear a sweater vest. And at the reveal, it would be revealed that the upstairs is perfect for my wife and kids and the basement will be perfect for him and me . . .


My Busy Agent phones. He tells me he can't talk but wants to know, do I want to meet on that project I said I didn't want to meet on but said I would think about? "Meet on"—makes it sound fancier than it is. I'm really like the guy filling out the job application at McDonald's. Both hoping to get the job and hoping *not* to get the job. Not wanting it, but upset when he doesn't get it.

My agent always has good news and bad news. "The good news is the last thing you pitched, three places wanted it. The bad news is, in the end, no one wanted it." He can always tell me where I am. Where I am *at*. Like some map he keeps in his head or in his office. Or like the pie chart he sends out of the Kids in the Hall, explaining who we are. And which one I am. I'm the dark purple slice because, apparently, I craft narratives Frank Zappa could not comprehend.

I ask, "Hold on, what was the response to the script we just sent out?"

"What script?" he wonders. "Oh, right, now I remember: the thing you spent most days of many months on . . . Well, I'm following up. Trading calls. Looking for traction. Can't talk. Gotta jump."

I make a mental note to look up the Spanish translation for "Nadia, we need to cut back your hours." (Later, I do look it up. It's *tenernos que reducir sus horas,* in case you ever need to know it.)

I like to freak my Busy Agent out. It is one of the few hobbies I have left. Like the time I had a very large and important martini around 5 p.m. (It's five o'clock somewhere. Yes, here at my house.) and phoned him and told him, in all seriousness, that the next thing I was passionate about writing was a children's book called *Angie, the HIV Unicorn.* You know? A cautionary but uplifting book for kids. He didn't smell money.

"You're not listening!" I said. "She's not full-blown, she only has the bug! Big difference." He didn't get it.

If I really want to unravel him, I just say the word "poem." He'll start to babble and blister. In Hollywood, there is something called a pilot season. But I don't think there is anything called a poem season. I've sprinkled a few throughout the following pages, just to piss him off.


I had kids late in life. It was like they were just putting the barstools up to close the place down and I ordered one for the road. Well, *two* for the road.

I have this game I play with my kids. I say to my daughter, Heidi, "What's your name again?" She says, "Heidi." I say, "What a coincidence, I have a daughter named Heidi!" "Dad! That's me." It's a redundant game, but I do it for a reason. That game is my Alzheimer's insurance.

Someday, not too long from now, I'll be slumped in a chair, mustard in the corner of my mouth, that mysterious white stuff in the other corner. The white stuff in the corners of old guys' mouths, I suspect it's marrow from their bones. I will wipe the white crud away, look at her and say, "What's your name again?" Hopefully she'll think we're just playing that silly game.

We also have a game called Daddy Can't Get Out of the Bathtub.

But in Hollywood, I'm practically a young dad.

In Hollywood, the men don't have trophy wives anymore, but rather trophy toddlers. The Hollywood Hills are filled with men who have children they stare at but cannot lift. Men so old, their kids will be able to beat them up as soon as they learn to walk. Men in thousand-dollar linen jackets still wearing Crocs (for some reason), picking their kids up at daycare, saying, "Which one is mine again?" They always take the wrong kid home. But there's a service that sorts it out. It's Hollywood.

In Hollywood, women get "the surgery." You know what I'm talking about, I'm sure. They get the surgery so they age only *inside* their bodies. Who cares about old organs and bones as long as your face looks young and fairly human at one particular angle?

They get the surgery so the tears they cry will flow beneath their faces. A silent river of tears. You can't see it, but you can hear it. If you listen closely late at night, as I always do, you can hear their tear glands at work. At first, you think it's coyotes. Nope. It's the sad hissing of sub-facial rivers that flow beneath the faces of former strippers, now mothers of three . . .

In Hollywood, a couple of months ago on my morning walk, I found something I just had to take a picture of:

The Hollywood Hills—where someone loses a teapot. How does one lose a teapot in the Hollywood Hills, exactly? It must be an important pot, because there's a big reward for it. My favourite detail is that people have pulled off the little phone number strips. There's a lot of activity around this teapot. The teapot is hot.

But aren't we all little lost teapots? I know I am.

Sometimes, I'll be in the middle of a pitch meeting and accidentally blurt out, "Who am I, Mommy?" And the enthusiastic, but distracted executives will look up from their notebooks. "What was the last part?" I'll catch myself and say, "Um . . . what I meant to say is . . . the characters are really active. Spinning plates. Raise the stakes!" "Oh, that sounds fantastic," and they go back to writing notes, which I always imagine are simply "pretend to be interested" or "have chicken for lunch."

Last week, perhaps the universe knew I was writing a book, because at the side of the road was this:

Wasn't that a party? Clearly, it was the baby who was drinking. Look at the size of the bottle. I can't figure out those headphones, though. What kind of music do babies listen to these days? I can't keep up.

I think this picture tells a classic Hollywood story: baby drives home drunk from the Viper Room, blaring loud music, doesn't hear the siren and, when he finally notices the flashing lights, shits himself.

See? Things never change in Hollywood.


I was in Hollywood a while back. Running on a literal, not figurative, treadmill. In my gym. I looked over, and the skinny introvert on the treadmill next to me was Eminem. I say this not to name-drop, but because there is a part you might find funny. In the row of treadmills behind your Rhyming Dark Eminence was his "security" walking on a treadmill of his own. This man, big and brawny as you would imagine, was surveying the room for signs of possible trouble. Would any of the pretty girls doing their abs while texting decide to pounce? What was he going to do? Chase someone on his treadmill, while that zany Muppets music played? This opportunity was too good to let slide, so

I turned to Eminem and glowered. Two can play your game, Marshall.

I found the one Eminem song I have on my iPod and cranked it into my headphones. Yes, I am going to use your music to inspire me to beat you. Ha! Alanis, *that's* what ironic means. Then I cranked up the speed of my treadmill to pass him. Without looking up from under his death-dark hoodie, Eminem upped his speed to match mine. And I can't be certain, but I think Security sped up on his treadmill to follow me too. It's on!

Legs pumping. My arms gauging circles, I felt youth coursing through my body. Like when I was seventeen, chasing imaginary antelope through the underbrush.

Demonstratively, I dabbed the well-earned sweat with the towel that's hung over the treadmill handlebars. As I expertly placed it back, it slipped. I looked down just in time to see it get tangled in my feet. I grunted embarrassingly as I fell shoulder-first onto the whizzing treadmill. My headphones ripped from my iPod, and the words to "The Real Slim Shady" played at full volume from my phone. Regrouping and ashamed, I looked back up, and Marshall's treadmill whizzed away mysteriously without him. He was gone.

There stood his Security, who turned off and wiped down Marshall's machine so he wouldn't have to be bothered dealing with his own sweat. Or, perhaps, so no one could steal it.

Oh, Hollywood.

# Angie, the HIV Unicorn

Hair as soft as feathers,

Feathers as soft as hair.

Unicorns have a rule,

Please don't touch me "there."


Yes, her name was Angie,

Practical and smart.

Never gave away her prize,

Was stingy with her heart.


Bad things always happen

Just before the pizza arrives.

You know it's a bad sign

When a guy's member is

Covered in flies.


Angie was feeling lonely,

So she gussied up her horn.

She flew into a party,

There, her ordeal was born.

And that's how she became,

Angie, our HIV unicorn.


He walked into the party,

His posse looking tight.

Ronald on his left,

Grimace on his right.


She knew him by his striped shirt,

She knew him by his mask.

They all knew that he'd be thieving

When they heard his cackling laugh.


Parties do turn ugly

When the hosts are watching porn.

Parties do turn ugly

When the Hamburglar

Is out chasing horn.


He sidled up to Angie,

Soothing in his drawl.

Pulled out his magic bong

Filled with propofol.


Unicorns are special,

But they can fall prey.

'Cuz instead of a condom,

He used a wrapper from a fish filet.

Oh Angie, you're our HIV unicorn.


You let yourself down, down, down

By getting so messed up.

You let yourself down, down, down,

Now you gotta get your T-cells up.


Listeners to my story,

Please don't have a fear,

For unicorns are magical creatures.

So if she takes the cocktail,

She'll live for five million years . . .

# *The Mouse and I*

My daughter, Heidi, is good at putting her hands on her hips and catching you doing things. Things that often you didn't even realize you were doing. Like aging.

"You're the oldest in the family. You'll probably die first," she recently pointed out.

"You never know," I offered vaguely as I made a mental date with myself to do some exercise.

Previous owners had renovated our starter mansion over the decades—on the cheap. It was never really built to last. But it did. We didn't think we were going to last in it, either. But we did.

In the interest of full disclosure, I must tell you that the house had already survived the "Rat Scare of 2012."

One night, as my Pretty Wife and I were sitting cuddled up on the corner couch watching *Masterpiece Classics*—or perhaps it was *Hoarders*—we heard a sound. A tiny, repetitive, demon-scratching coming from the kitchen. Heroically, I thrust on some oven mitts and grabbed a pot and a knife. She rolled up one of her catalogues. Much more deadly.

Together, we went hunting.

Then I heard a little telltale noise. I knew exactly where it was.

"Sweetie, I think it is in this cupboard. I will face it. But in the meantime," I said, pointing to the cupboard it was *actually* in, "why don't you check out *that* cupboard?"

She fell for it. Opened the door and there it was. At eye level, eating a whole piece of melba toast. She slammed the door, yelped, dry-heaved and said, "I stared right into the eyes of a rat. I feel like I have been eye-raped."

"Oh, sweetie," I mourned, "it should have been me."

We tossed and turned that night, knowing a rat was some-where in the walls. In the morning, I sprang into action. I authorized the unlimited use of my credit cards. Men with vans were dispatched.

To defend my soiled wife, I requested the "cruellest traps

money can buy," which turned out to be heavy-duty Kevlar units, fireproof (for some reason) and featuring a steel kill mechanism. I felt giddy as they were set.

Breathlessly, we waited.

Days later, a few lumps in sacks were carted off by men whose world-weary eyes told me they had seen too much. Then I demanded that the house be totally sealed. Putty and wire were put around the periphery. Every hole, real or imagined, was obliterated. The exterior was wind- and water-tested. Our starter mansion became a fortress. Nothing could get in.

But last fall, my wife decided I needed a new desk. She just "happened to see" a great one online. Suspicious, I know, how she had just "happened to see one," when we had agreed not to shop for anything for the "foreseeable future." She saw the desk and nabbed it—at a very good price for, as she later confessed, a desk of "that quality."

I came home from being out of the house, and there sat a jumbo desk.

I said, "Why don't you and Nadia (our housekeeper) carry it up and I will supervise?"

My wife said no, Nadia should watch the children. So Nadia

watched the children watch my wife and me carry it up. *Smash*. A small window broke. It was my fault, but really, it was Nadia's, you know?

Heidi pointed out that we had broken a window and we must get it replaced. Angrily, I covered the hole with cardboard and gaffer's tape. Actual gaffer's tape given to me by a gaffer, as arguably, I was still in the business. Heidi helped me tape up the hole. Roscoe helped by pouring me a drink.

The next morning, I began my daily duties, starting with getting Heidi her first apple-in-a-bowl of the day, when, out of the corner of my eye, I saw a small shadow dart by. My blood froze.

"What's wrong?"

"Nothing," I lied.

Searing music played as I moved towards the cardboard window. A small hole stared back at me. The house was a fortress. Nothing could get in, which meant nothing could get out. We were now living with a mouse. I closed the hole up quickly before anyone could see.

I wanted to tell my wife, but I couldn't. All day, I walked around in a fog. Like Tiger Woods waiting for the mistresses to call. I knew something was going to happen, I just didn't know when.

That night, my wife and I were on the couch, watching *House*

*Hunters International,* and it was just getting good when we heard a sound in the kitchen. A small rustling in the cupboard.

"Oh, I think I saw a moth go in there," I said. "Do you want to look while I check on the children? They are so important to me, and I forgot to kiss them good night."

She fell for it. Again. This was like Charlie Brown and the football.

I darted around the corner, but doubled back because I really wanted to see my wife see the mouse. Then she screamed. I rushed in and she told me there was a mouse!

"A mouse?" I repeated. I went over and inspected the little mouse hole in the cardboard.

"I never should have let Heidi tape this up."

"Don't blame yourself," said my Pretty Wife.

"You're right. That would be unfair to me."

As we talked, it became clear that she didn't mind the mouse living with us. They are kind of cute, so why not let it stay? I thought this was a terrible idea. Mice creep me out. I realized I had to get rid of the mouse—on my own. Behind everyone's back.

The next night, as I sipped the "discreet Shiraz" Roscoe had suggested, I mentally rehearsed my plan. In my knapsack, beneath the sweaty gym clothes that no one would dare venture past, was a mousetrap. I planned to set it the moment my wife went to bed, then get up early and dispose of the mouse before she stirred. Also, for the sake of full disclosure, I thought it would be fun for my wife to still think she was living with a mouse even after it was long gone. She's even prettier when she's frazzled. But I digress. I blame Roscoe, who had left me with a freshly decanted bottle.

My wife went off to bed. I sneaked over to my sweat sack and out came the trap. A little tipsy, I put peanut butter in it and set it. Hyperventilating from stress, I ran back to bed. Hyperventilating in a way that made my wife wake up and think I was giving her "the signal." Not great timing, but what the heck? Writers can't be choosers.

She groaned as she took off her Lululemon yoga pants and underwear. She flipped on her back. We started making sweet love—me doing all the work. As with my writing and pitching of shows, my wife's part is to hope and endure.

About fifty lashes in, I heard a distinctive snap coming from the kitchen. The trap had been sprung. I want to say I stopped immediately, but in truth, I kept going with increased vigour, now understanding the thrill of the hunter.

At first light, I shook awake and ran to my quarry. There it was: a tiny mouse beneath an overturned trap. A writer might describe it as looking like "the Wicked Witch of the West underneath a blood-and-innards-covered house." I grabbed a plastic bag and bagged it. As I turned, there stood Heidi, hands on hips.

"What do you have in the bag?"

To make things worse, she shone a small Curious George flashlight at me, then at the bag.

"Oh, nothing at all," I said, lying badly.

When she tried to look inside, I employed one of the world's lamest magic tricks: I opened the bag, but didn't let her see the purple surprise at the bottom. I thought I'd got away with it. But Heidi turned to my arriving wife and said, "Mom, Dad has a dead mouse in that bag."

Over the next couple of days, my wife turned on me. How could I trap a mouse so inhumanely? A fan of the underdog, she started siding with the mouse.

"What if it was a mother? What if it was pregnant?"

"Well," I thought, "we got her just in time."

My wife was now certain that it was a female. Alone and misunderstood, not unlike herself. Flipping through catalogues looking for *herself*. Okay, I added that last part.

As a cruel coincidence, Roscoe had been cast as a mouse in the upcoming school play.

"Do you have something against your own son?" she demanded.

Before I could answer, she vowed to park the accusation until our next couples therapy session.

"What a party that'll be," I muttered.

Things were tense that night as we went to bed. Even precious Roscoe was no help. The martini I had been teaching him to make for me was terrible. It took a couple more tries before he got it right and was allowed to go to bed.

I lay there, sweating and restless. I was hyperventilating. But trust me, the Lululemon pants and their companion panties remained welded tightly to my Pretty Wife.

It was cold in that bed.

Then we heard a little scratching outside the window. And a faint little sound, almost like moaning. Like a little mouse. A tiny, heartbroken mouse, trying to get in, no matter the cost. "Her husband," my wife said angrily. And finally, the fight gates opened up.

"How could you kill a wife and a mother?"

"Do you know how hard I work?"

"If it were me that was missing, would you even try to rescue me?"

"I'm tired of turning out lights all the time. Do you know how expensive electricity is?"

I lost that fight and then the next few. I had trouble explaining to the Outline People why the outline for the TV show I was writing was late. But we kept hearing "him" at night, pining for "her" as I apparently never would.

That Tuesday at couples therapy, they decided—I mean, *we* decided—that we must call the expensive rat catcher and bring back the vans. He would need to figure out a way to let the mouse husband in and catch him humanely. And then take him somewhere . . . The last part of the plan was fuzzy.

So we called up the exterminator. A hole was opened and a little merciful trap was set. He didn't want to do it this way, but I was adamant. I was a man in charge, who wasn't doing any of the actual work. At my insistence, a small camera was installed. Just to make sure.

The next morning, the smug bastard reported a miracle. He showed us the footage, thinking it would be more "effective." I almost threw up in my oatmeal. We had let in over a hundred mice. They were now asleep in the walls. A hundred snaps of a hundred traps lay ahead of me.

# Pyjama-Rama

Ever feel like you were once young and cool and then you woke up in the middle of your life, emptying the dishwasher? I do. I'm getting older, and suddenly, I understand the appeal of golf. It's the only sport where the fans resemble the players. Also, I'm starting to check the weather. In other cities. I don't know anybody in these cities. I'm not going to them. But for some reason, I feel I need to know.

Now, when I'm in a restaurant and the food arrives, I feel compelled to take a picture of it. Why? Age, I'm told. I believe I'm turning into one of those old men standing there, waiting for the bank to open. Running home to talk on my land line and looking forward to the most exciting moment of my day: when the mailman comes.

Here's something I've been finding myself doing: in the middle of the day, I change my socks for a little "pick-me-up." And by the way, it really works. Go try it. I'll wait . . . See? Don't you feel more vim?

I don't keep my "skinny jeans" anymore as motivation to hit the gym and get in great shape. I keep them in case I get cancer. Cancer pants.

I have old-fashioned taste in women. I like the women in shampoo ads *before* they wash their hair. I like that dirty, clumpy hair. I don't find it lifeless. I find it life-affirming and lovely. Also, I like the women in the weight-loss ads before they've lost the weight. That too-tight one-piece? The surly scowl on her face? Much sexier than the new chirpy girl who's lost sixty-six pounds in sixty-seven days.

Feminist or Lothario? Tweet topic. Do people live-tweet books? I don't really know how it works.

We were gentlemen once. Now it's all, "Girl, bring that boda-cious backside over here and shake it at me like a salt shaker." Back then, we might say, "I love the way your haircut flatters your face." Which really meant, "I want to make love to you, first gently, and then cruelly, like you were a rag doll." But we *talked* like gentlemen. We were feminists. Or at least we would *say* we were feminists to have our way with women. Then, in the morning, we would quietly reveal that we'd slept with them in part to shower and use their shampoo and Q-Tips. The women kind of expected it, forgave you and made you breakfast. Gentler times.

There was no porn when I was growing up. Yes, I created the occasional erotic Lite-Brite picture. I believe the set came with so many pink lights for that very purpose. Or we'd draw a dirty Etch-a-Sketch. If your mom walked in, you could just shake it really fast, obliterating the evidence. Now there is porn everywhere. A little while ago, I was working away on my computer, and up popped all this "lactation porn." Just because I typed in the phrase "lactation porn."

Part of getting older is remembering. At some point, and you don't know exactly when, you have more life behind you to remember than ahead of you to live.

As a young punk, I used to wear pyjamas ironically. Now I just wear them. I work in my pyjamas. Sometimes, in the middle of the day, for no reason, I change out of my pyjamas and into other pyjamas. Like with the socks, energized, I go back to doing whatever it was I was doing.

The first time you leave the house in your PJs, it's exhilarating.

Just to get in the car and sail off to mail a letter, you feel so free. You wonder, "What has been holding me back for so long?" Then, pyjamas on, you dart out, down the hill to the Starbucks drive-thru. Smile at the guy working the window. Look at his nametag. Use his name. Get your coffee. I got away with it!

Then, you think, "I suppose I can run into the store to get the asparagus my Pretty Wife needs." By the way, where I come from, no one ever *needed* asparagus. Eventually, you say to yourself, "Of course I can wear my pyjamas to the doctor; I could be sick. I'm not, but I could be." Then you realize it's not illegal to wear them to an 11 a.m. movie. Or why not wear them when I receive the prestigious "One of the 100,000 Best Comedians from Canada Now Working in the United States" award?

Wearing pyjamas in public. It's one of those things that you feel in your heart may be wrong, but you aren't sure why. Like masturbating in front of your dog. By the way, I mean *accidentally* masturbating in front of your dog. Like, you are feeling the need to interfere with yourself and you look over . . . and there is your dog. So you think, "Well, I've already started. I might as well finish." That's what my life coach would want me to do. I'm not talking about chasing your dog around going, "Hey Buddy, look at this! Look at what I can do and you can't. Yippee!"

•••

I had a dream recently where my son was firing me. "Dad, got a minute? We need to make some changes." But then, as he was firing me, it became clear that he had no idea what my job was. Ha! So, Roscoe, who gets the last laugh? I pointed out that if he didn't know what I did, how was he going to replace me?

My children don't know what I do for a living. I think it's a bad sign when I have to keep reminding them. And when I do, they sort of don't believe me.

So when it was Career Day at my children's school, I was impressed. Roscoe wanted to go dressed as a hipster.

"Like Dad," he said.

I don't know where he even got the notion. I thought, "Yes, son, become a hipster. Like Daddy. Like Daddio. Someone who drinks in beat poetry and free thought. Someone who questions and searches as he cuts a creative swath through the world." But it turns out Roscoe thought a hipster was someone who hung around the house all day in his pyjamas and watched TV. He explained this to his class, and they found it hilarious. Also, when he was asked to draw a picture of his family for class, I was wearing pyjamas and had a TV remote tucked under my chin (as, truthfully, I sometimes do) and a drink in my hand (as, truthfully, I sometimes do). Ms. Ocean, his kindergarten teacher, sent me a concerned email. Meaning, one not riddled with happy faces and exclamation marks for a change!!!

So when someone from school asked me to host "Pyjama-Rama," how could I say no? I was already dressed for it. Pyjama-Rama, "a fundraiser with an emphasis on fun." I thought this was a good chance to show my kids what I did for a living. As I had done on my silly-skit show: make people laugh.

These gigs are always harder than they look. Especially for me. I'm an acquired taste, not a crowd-pleaser. Just ask my wife. I'm not an ages-eight-to-eighty talent. Perhaps more like ages eight *or* eighty.

On show night, my Pretty Wife, Roscoe, Heidi and I walked up to the school as a proud pyjama-clad family. There was excitement in the air. My daughter was holding my hand. Squeezing my hand. I realized she was nervous. Not for herself, because she had to be around all the "big kids" in sixth grade, but because she was worried for me. About how I might do.

"I think Daddy knows exactly what he's doing," I boasted.

But as I said that, something like nerves shot through me. Also, some of those sixth-graders did look pretty rough. A few were bigger than me. Whatever. I was going to be fine, I told myself. I had performed for some pretty rough crowds. Rowdy drunks and, even scarier, a fundraiser for a sober-living facility.

As I came onstage, I wasn't really sure what to do first. Anyone who has had the cruel misfortune of working with me will tell you, this can be dangerous. I get weird by default. Or perhaps I just allow myself to be as weird as I am. The first thing I said was, "I like pyjamas. But of course, I support the troops." Silence.

"The troops don't have the luxury to sit around in their pyjamas, do they?"

Confused faces of all ages stared up at me. Of course, I changed the topic immediately—no, I did not! I doubled down on this satirical riff.

"So let's give a big hand for the troops who are fighting for our freedom. Who are not free to wear pyjamas themselves, as they must wear helmets and bulky bulletproof vests. Shall we pass the hat, to send the troops pillow pets?" Confused applause.

Cue music: I sang and danced, "I put my hands up in the air sometimes. Join me." Few joined me. What comedian can't make kids laugh by silly-dancing? Well, one that had said some weird things prior to attempting it.

I tried not to look at my family, just in case things got worse.

But how could they? I still had my "killer stuff" ahead of me. Or what I had thought would be my killer stuff. I tried a piece where I asked the principal up so she and I could act out the "Hot for Teacher" video by Van Halen. (I re-watched it in my office as preparation. It actually holds up better than you would think.) But when I tried it with her, it sort of fell apart. But in my own defence, she was no help. Too old for the part, and definitely not a natural.

Realizing I was in free fall, I quipped, "The black and whites are going to come and haul me off the stage." Then I realized that the phrase "black and whites" might have a racial connotation, and not be understood as the black-and-white police cruisers I had intended. Great. Here I was, starting a race riot at my children's school. I locked eyes with Heidi. Her dad, a middle-aged man in his flop sweat–filled tartan pyjamas, a man that perhaps she didn't even understand.

She looked up at me and shouted, "My dad thinks that poo is beautiful."

Big laugh. It might have appeared like I was being heckled by a family member, but I wasn't.

I feel I need to explain. My wife and I had been very cognizant of not instilling our body issues in our children. I mean, here

I stand, a man with a smallish frame and a jumbo head. It's a marvel that I can even walk. I have beady little sunken eyes and tiny hamster hands. When I undress, a multitude of problems are revealed. And according to the Internet, I am only seventeen inches tall. So I know firsthand how one's body image can affect someone. (Luckily, my legs are "quite perfect" and have gotten me into many VIP rooms.) So in an effort not to have Heidi feel "poo shame," I had been forced into a conversation where I told her, "Everything about your body is beautiful."

"Even poo?" she probed.

"Yes, I guess you have me there. Even poo."

The next day at school, as the class lined up, Heidi blurted out, "My dad thinks poo is beautiful!" Everyone laughed. Everyone except me, the other parents and the teachers. I tried desperately to explain to them that, no, I wasn't some poo freak from Canada who was living amongst them. It wasn't a great moment in my human history.

What Heidi had remembered, though, was that there had been a big laugh. And now that I was having trouble on stage, she was trying to get that laugh again. To help me. So what I did was something I should do more often: nothing. I just stood there. And for some reason, I got a huge, life-affirming laugh.

I'd had a bad start, followed by a slow middle, but at least I ended well.

After the show, I stood with my Pretty Wife, Roscoe and Heidi, who was beaming because she knew she had helped me. A couple of young parents walked up.

The goateed husband said, "Wow, man that was awesome. The things you said about the U.S.A. being in bullshit wars? Not everyone got it, but we did."

I smiled and shrugged at my family as if to say, "Hey, it's what I do. I'm a hipster."

# False Teeth

My sense of travel I learned from a boozer: my dad. He'd say, "Go west, young man, stop at the fridge and bring me back a beer." My dad was a boozer and a salesman. The better he was at one, the worse he was at the other.

I learned my sense of the great outdoors from being locked out of the house. Or should I say, townhouse? The one with the cedar shingles on the outside and the people yelling on the inside. Or as they are sometimes referred to, a family. Growing up where I did, a "water feature" was a garden hose and a "liquor cabinet" was a bottle under the sink, always in need of replacing.

My dad had these false teeth that he clicked whenever he has angry. Which was always. He'd bob his teeth up and down and glare at you. He had an operation scar that snaked across his chest. This was in the old days, when they still did operations for ulcers. If I had such a scar, I would never take my shirt off. He never had one on. All he ever wore were these baggy plaid shorts that always sprouted his plumber's crack. Or in his case, a salesman's crack, which is even scarier.

Just as I now have games I play with my kids, I had games with him. Starting around age eight, after he was out for a "long night," my older sister and I would play "Find Daddy's Car." We would check all the places he might have stopped. Well, bars where he might have drunk. Sort of a scavenger hunt.

We were given two dimes. One to call him from a pay phone when we located his car, and the second dime for "expenses"— licorice for keeping our mouths shut. It was a charade. My mom always knew what we were up to. But she looked the other way. That was the game that *she* played.

Then, later in the day, my sister, Dad and I would play "Hibernation." He'd pretend to be a bear. And sleep. We would be the "baby bears" that would lie with him. Or watch him. It was some years later that I realized he'd started this game for the raw, uninterrupted sleep. But truthfully, to this day, I am comforted by the sound of someone snoring. Because it always means they are not dead.

One time after a Grey Cup party, I had to drive us home. The problem was, I was only ten. The Calgary Stampeders had lost. Again. So my dad had been hitting the rye and ginger pretty hard. But in all fairness, he would have done that if they'd won, so I don't blame the Stamps. It was time to go home. He and I got into his Chrysler Cordoba.

He pulled out, but then he slammed on the brakes. "I can't do it, Bruce. I'm lit like a firecracker. You're going to have to drive us home."

"I'm ten, Dad."

"Exactly. You need to learn how to drive. No time like the present."

I got out, then slid in behind the wheel. I could barely see over the convex dashboard. I remember thinking, "They won't make me go to jail 'cause I'm a kid. If my dad told me to drive, then I had to do it, right?"

As my dad lit a cigarette, I turned up the radio. The rock station, CKXL, because now I was in charge. (I'm guessing a song by Blood, Sweat & Tears blasted out.) I located the blinker, then put the shifter in *D* and pulled out onto the street. "Wow," I screamed to no one in particular, and definitely not my dad, as I moved past parked cars. He watched for a minute, then leapt from his seat and pulled the emergency brake.

"You've got a lot to learn. And when you *do* learn to drive, never drive drunk." With that, he slid back into the driver's seat and drove us home.

One summer, my father dragged us away from our friends and up to the cottage. The cottage was one of the few places I remember having fun with him. He'd actually come outside.

He'd swim with us in the lake. It was all good until, one time, he cannonballed off the dock, screaming,"Woo-hoo!" His false teeth wobbled, then flew out of his head. He tried to grab them as he submerged. Water filled his mouth. Seconds later, he came up, and his mouth was half-empty. He was without his top dentures.

"I can't find them," he whistled. We laughed, thinking he was trying to be funny, but he wasn't. Nope, he had lost his teeth, and now it was *our* problem. My sister's and mine. My mom retreated back the cottage, always the smartest of the bunch.

My father whistled for all the kids from the surrounding cottages to gather 'round. He announced that he'd give five bucks to whoever found them. That was big money in those days. (You're right, still is.) But I didn't want to find them for the money; I wanted to help my dad. I mean, it's hard enough to be a salesman at the best of times, but c'mon, even Willy Loman had teeth. I didn't want my dad to be further humiliated than the thousand times he'd already been in his life, so I led the hunt.

The other kids and I scoured the lake, looking for his missing chompers. Me with the mask and snorkel I used to play with in the bathtub for hours. All that practice would certainly pay off. I thought, if I was good at anything, it was probably this. My sister, not a natural swimmer, ran back to the cottage to make some cardboard signs: "Missing Teeth. Big Reward."

We bobbed in the lake till the sun was setting. It was getting cold. The other kids got tired and gave up. I stayed behind. I wanted to be a hero. And sometimes being a hero means pulling teeth from a murky Manitoba lake long past dusk. I dove down under the pier, grabbing handfuls of mud. Finally, I felt something. I'd done it! I'd found them! I surfaced and opened up my hand—it was a Mountain Dew can.

"Well," I announced, "it's a good sign. It means they can't be far." Which obviously makes no sense.

I stayed in that lake till I turned blue. Then my sister came back to get me. It was time to give up.

Meanwhile, my dad had been back at the cottage, brooding. And by brooding, I mean drinking. My mother and sister had left in Mom's car. You see, my parents had a silent pact to always drive separately. That way, if there was an accident, at least one parent and child would survive. So I got Dad. Lucky me. He told me there was no time to change—I could do it back at home, in an hour or so, which at that age, seemed perfectly reasonable.

We hopped into the car, me still in my wet bathing suit and my Tony the Tiger towel. We rode home in silence, aside from the occasional squeal of the tires as my dad "corrected" the drifting car.

And then I heard it: the sound of a siren. We were getting pulled over.

The cop walked up, the terrible echoing footsteps.

He asked my dad, "Do you know why I pulled you over?"

My dad muttered a bad joke about him fulfilling a "quota" by giving us a bogus ticket.

"Nope," explained the cop, "speeding."

Then my dad said, no, it was the cop who was speeding. In

fact, my dad said, he might have to make a citizen's arrest on him. A citizen's arrest on a cop. See what I survived?

The cop said, "Sir, you're slurring your words. Have you been drinking?"

As people always say in these situations, "No. I've only had one glass of wine."

He'd never had a glass of wine in his life. Maybe ten glasses of rye. Or some vodka in a wineglass. But never wine.

The cop wasn't buying it.

I blurted out, "No, he sounds funny because of his teeth. He lost them."

My dad sheepishly smiled at the cop. Giving him the full gums. I held up one of the three crude reward posters my sister had made. The cop looked at it as if it had some bearing on the case. "Hmm . . ."

Into that terrible lull, I blurted, "And the honest truth, Sir . . . I peed my pants."

He stared at me. I motioned to the towel over my wet bathing suit, which made peeing my pants seem possible.

"Oops, I should go to the potty sooner," I said, trying to sound three years old.

Playing along, my father said, "I told the kid umpteen times to go to the toilet before we got in the car."

"Yeah, Dad. But you didn't tell me how many times umpteen was." The cop stared. The joke sunk in, and he laughed.

Handing my father back his licence, he said, "You should get that boy home, before he craps himself, too."

It worked. I was, for one day in my long life, a hero.

# Hello, Goodbye

"I made it with a tall girl once. It took all night. It wasn't the
act that took the time, but the convincing."

When you're eleven, you don't know what to do to grow up. Except, perhaps, wait. So I just combed my hair, hoping my body would catch up with my slightly older-looking hair. I combed my hair a lot. Like, a *lot*. As soon as one side was done, the other side needed doing again. I think I put a thousand miles on that wide-toothed comb that I kept in the back pocket of my baby-blue cords.

The first time I went to a preteen dance, it was odd because my family actually encouraged me. Like I've learned that families are supposed to do. Who knew? My parents even gave me their advice.

"Always say, 'It would be my privilege to have this next dance,' and lead her to the very middle of the dance floor," my father said.

"And after, say 'thanks' while looking her directly in the eye," my mother chimed in.

As I made my way out the door, my sister pulled me aside. Which was hard to do, because our townhouse was really small.

She asked, "Don't you want my advice?"

"I don't know. Do I?"

She surveyed my dickey, which I hadn't tucked inside my shirt. My first punk act. Tucking my dickey inside my mustard-coloured paisley shirt, she said, "If you wanna score tonight, listen to me."

Score? I was eleven.

"If you get a chance to kiss a girl, don't blow into her mouth."

"Why would I blow into her mouth?"

"Exactly," she replied. "And don't push her lips. Pull her lips with yours. Lure her. That's the way to land her. Then you'll have her all night."

I pretended to understand that nonsense she had just told me.

Last thing. "Here, take this." She pulled out a cigarette. "It'll freshen your breath. It's menthol. Smoke it before you go inside. Then keep a little smoke in your lungs, in case . . ." Unconvinced, I stared at the cigarette.

"Trust me," she said. I took it. Tucked it into my back pocket beside my comb.

Music played as I walked into the school gymnasium. It felt so, dare I say, sexy in half-light. The bleachers shadowed romantically. No one mindlessly running laps. No one throwing a dodge ball at my head. But then I realized it was full of teenage boys. At a preteen dance? I should've known. It's what men have been doing since the dawn of time: trolling for younger women. I looked around at all the thirteen-year-olds with full beards who had rolled up on their mini-bikes.

I stood there awkwardly. I didn't know what to do first. I air-guitared half-heartedly, pretending to get lost in the music so I wouldn't seem so lonely. I only seemed like a freak. Then I air-guitared and combed my hair. Then I just air-combed my hair.

A cruel science teacher, hair sprouting from his ears—you know the type—was making his rounds. He was on "boner patrol." Not letting you dance if you had one. But it was early; the last slow song of the night was a long way off. There were no boners yet. But he was also trolling for dope. Booze. Penknives.

He stopped and pointed at my back pocket and snapped, "What do you have in there?"

"Nothing," I said.

Then, as he went to check, I remembered the cigarette under the comb. I did the worst magic trick of all time and crushed the cigarette down into my pocket as I retrieved the comb.

"Just a comb for my beautiful hair." Hoping the bravado of "beautiful hair" might somehow throw him off the hunt. As a demonstration, I combed my hair. In the gym's half-light, he failed to see the tobacco flecks that I combed throughout.

After a long night of being all alone and pretending I was interested in what I was doing, I was exhausted. Things hadn't really gone my way. Then they put on the song that everyone knew would be the last song of the night: "Hello, Goodbye" by the Beatles. People scrambled to pair up. The teenagers with pube-mustaches plucked the prettiest ten- and eleven-year-olds. Soon everyone had a partner. And, of course, I mean, everyone but me.

I wanted to sneak out, but then, as the bodies came together, I saw her. Standing by the basketball hoop, where I think she could usually be found. An extremely tall girl. Her name was

Jane. Jane Melonoski, if you think you need to know. But I'm not sure why you would.

She galloped over, then stopped and got suddenly shy, her large frame transformed into that of a sweet little girl.

She said, "Wanna?" Which was the sexiest thing I'd heard in my life up until then.

But wait: it gets sexier. My "training" kicked in. I said, "It would be my privacy." Which was obviously supposed to be "privilege." Oh well. My hand disappeared into Jane's as I led her to our dance spot. We bodychecked a few people out of the way to get to the very centre of the dance floor. This seemed very natural to Jane, and I'm sure she had the trophies to prove it. Then she put her arms around my waist. Realizing it was a little low for her, she readjusted them to around my neck. That's better.

Then she brought me into her. I could smell her skin, the Herbal Essence shampoo in her hair. Good thing the boner police were nowhere in sight. Jane didn't know what I was going through because my "little baby-blue corduroy tent" landed just above her knee.

To this day, I still think "Hello, Goodbye" is the greatest song of all time because I danced with a tall girl to it.

Once the song was over, I walked her back to the basketball hoop and looked her straight in the eye, as I'd been told to do, and said, "Thank you." I kept staring. She thought this meant something more. She leaned down, took my "beautiful hair" in her meaty hands and kissed me. Without breathing into her mouth, I tried to pull her lips back with mine, thus "landing" her. It was no *Old Man and the Sea*, but our lips *did* touch, making it a legal kiss.

Then she said the best thing I had ever heard in my life: "Maybe next time?" Which meant, of course, there would be a next time. Maybe not with her. But in my life. For an instant, I was worried that I now had something I'd heard about, called VD. But that dumb thought was replaced by sheer joy.

Then another girl came up. She was cute, in a smart-girl kind of way. She smiled at me. What was happening? Had I crossed over? Was I now suddenly desirable because I was a kisser?

She asked, "Do you want to come hang out with us?"

I looked at her, and for some reason said, "No, I'm needed at home."

With that, I ran. I bolted out of the gym and ran all the way home. Seven, eight blocks. I huffed through the preteen night because I wanted to be home. I think I'd never run that fast or freely before. Or since. It was the only time I remember running to my house. I'd always run away from it. I still do.

But that night, when I got home, there was a miracle. My family was there, waiting for me. No one was drunk. No one was yelling. The TV wasn't even on. They turned, open-faced, and asked me how it went.

"Pretty good. I kissed a tall girl."

My dad glanced at his watch and deadpanned, "It took you long enough."

"Yeah, it took all night . . ."

My sister beamed. "I told you to trust me . . ."

# Never Trust

Never,

Never trust,

Never trust a man

Who says, "Trust me."


Never paint your face

With the name of your local sports team,

Unless they're playing.

Never name-drop

Your own name.

Never take a date to couple's therapy,

Saying, "How can she be part of the problem?

I just met her."


Never say, "Hey, I can kill a kid.

It's my birthday."

Never say, "It's my birthday," either.

If people don't know,

Then just shut up, Jack.


This guy called me up one time

In the middle of the night.

He told me he couldn't finish my roof

Because he lost his tools

To his ex-wife.


Never trust a roofer without work boots.

Never go up to a blind man,

Offering rippled chips,

Saying, "Here. Read these."

Never put your dog's X-rays on top of yours

To see what it would look like

If your dog

Lived inside of you.


Never describe yourself as

"A long-gone daddy with fists of steel

and a nose for trouble"

When the border guard asks,

"What you do for a living?"

Never say you're an actor, either.


I knew this cat one time,

His girl said she was on the pill.

It turned out the pill she was talking about

Was a little round sucker called

Advil.


Never trust a woman who uses a dream catcher

As a birth-control device.

Never trust a man who wants to start a family

"Right away."

Never go through a baby-name book,

Looking for the name

Of the child

You will never have.


Never plan your own intervention,

Saying, "I need to tell you all,

How my drinking,

Is affecting me!"


Never wear a wedding dress to another woman's wedding,

Saying it's merely a "tribute."

Never be at a funeral and say,

"You're next!"

Then "tink" your glass.


Never,

Never trust,

Never trust a man.

Never trust a man

Who repeats himself.

# The Beautiful Day You Beat Up Your Dad

Things change quickly when you have kids. My Doors T-shirt was replaced by a Dora one a long time ago.

Being a dad means always working. Always moving. Being a dad is never not having something in your hands and two thoughts in your head. One of those thoughts always being "Get thing for kid."

Your kids have no idea how hard you work for them.

I asked Roscoe one day, "Do you ever think about me when you're at school?"

Confusion crossed his face. "Why would I do that?"

To him, I am just this encouraging sap who's always been there; open arms, wallet and heart. He used to think I was cool. Now he's starting to suspect I am stupid. I can see it in his eyes. It won't be long now. One day soon, he is going to try and pound me down.


Growing up, taking on your old man is practically a rite of passage. Perhaps, for women, it's splashing white wine in your mom's face. Or maybe it's wearing her cocktail dress and looking better in it than she does? I'm not sure.

As young boys, my friends and I would often muse aloud about "the beautiful day you beat up your dad." We'd dream about how we would do it. Club him with his golf clubs? Yes. Club him with his own clubs. The pure ironic poetry of that appealed to us. Or maybe we'd drown him in his Old Spice, which he splashed on like a drunken sailor. Guillotine him with the garage door? Or simply fall on him from a tree as he came home from work—let gravity do the ass whooping.

Obviously, there are a lot of great options. As for me, I wasn't sure how I was going to do it. I only knew it needed to be done.

The beautiful day that you beat up your dad is very different, I have learned, from the beautiful day you *think* you are going to beat up your dad.

It was a Friday. I was at the dinner table, enjoying a new delicacy I had just invented called "bacon tasties"—I'd throw a piece of bacon into my mouth, then squirt back some ketchup, followed by a quick spoonful of mayonnaise—voilà. I'd only had about five of these treat sensations when he told me to stop it. It was "time."

Time to take out the garbage. The old bastard was obsessive about the garbage. How it needed to taken out when it was full. Not the day after. Or the day after that. In response, I'd begun opening the front door and just chucking it in the general direction of the garbage can. But no, that wasn't good enough for the old detail freak. He started following me out, making sure I did a "good job."

"I'll show you a good job," I thought to myself, "of beating the shit out of you!"

That winter day, he followed me out, shirtless and stupid, as always. I thought, "I am going to beat the shit out of my dad today and the world is going to thank me for it. This will be the greatest achievement of my young life."

I knew I needed to catch him off guard. The best way to do that was to pretend to be nice.

"Dad," I said "I need your advice on something . . ."

It worked. He softened, turned to me, looking almost human for an instant. Then I screamed and swung the engorged bag, full force. But adrenaline had gotten the better of me. The garbage was lighter than I had calculated. I swung and missed him entirely. I fell into the snowbank. He stood over me and clicked his teeth, taunting me.

Instinctively, I hocked a loogie up at his smirking, puffy face. But again, I had miscalculated. I was on the ground, so the gob went up in the air, stopped and, I think, hovered. Perhaps it even looked back at me and shook its head before landing on my face. My neck. My beautiful rock hair. This would not be the beautiful day I beat up my dad.

It happened the next autumn. I was thirteen then. Another summer of blow-drying my hair had made my arms strong. I was ready. I told myself that the next time my dad turned down my music, he would die.

The plan was simple: I would lure him into my bedroom with rock music, then pound him. As he bent over to turn down the stereo, I would grab a handful of his armpit jowl and squeeze till he cried. Then I would swing the metal TV tray I ate my meals off of, hitting him in the head. He'd collapse like a sack of potatoes onto the shag rug. I imagined stepping on his throat with my Adidas Tobaccos and screaming, "Stay down, old man!" I was most looking forward to hiding the body beneath the beanbag chair. Then, the glory.

It was eight in the morning. I removed the Eggos from the TV tray. Good; now I could swing it unencumbered. I turned off *Rocket Robin Hood*. I put on my favourite record that year, *Quadrophenia* by The Who. I put on side one. Not the first cut, of course—"I Am the Sea" starts too slowly. I put on the second cut, "The Real Me." I thought, "Can't you see the real me, Daddy?" So I put on the record. And waited.

Soon, I heard him lumber towards my door. The predictable lummox, coming to his slaughter.

But he didn't just throw the door open, as he usually did. He actually knocked. Which caught me off guard. As I relaxed the TV tray momentarily, I noticed he had shaving cream on his face.

"Perfect," I thought. "It will make it all the funnier when the story is retold through the generations."

"Not bad," he said, referring to the music. "The bass is pretty good."

"Entwistle. He's only the best bass player in the world, Dad!"

He leaned over the stereo. This was my moment. But he actually turned it up. Then he listened for a minute. Even through the shaving cream, I could see him smile.

"I better shave. Then I'll drive you to school, okay?"

With that, he left. I had missed my moment. I had not planned for the rarest of all human possibilities, that the old bastard would wake up in a good mood.

Afterwards, I lay there. Listening to the bass. I would not be beating my dad up that day. In fact, I never did.

By the time I was old enough and strong enough to trounce him, I didn't want to anymore. I was busy. Anyway, as it turned out, his life ended up doing it for me.

The cruel irony is that in the last few years, I had to take care of him. It happened slowly. I don't think anyone ever handed me the keys to the family, saying, "Here. You drive." After the first time I paid for my dad's lunch, he never paid again. I didn't know then that I was on the slow path to me being in charge. Lunch at Golden Griddle would one day become me cutting his toenails because he couldn't anymore.

In the end, your parents become your children. One day, you'll be feeding your parents applesauce and tucking them in and telling them what to do. So when you look at your parents, really, you're looking at your children. And when you look at your children, you are looking at the kids who will one day take care of you.

In your nightmares, as the plane lumbers silently down from the heavens to crash into a mountain, or perhaps less poetically, into a Canadian Tire parking lot—in that painful fantasy, you don't long for yourself. You don't mourn the rest of the life you didn't have. You think only of your kids who will wander around lost and angry after they blow the insurance money.

That's being a parent. That's being a dad. Your life is less important than the thing living with you, who, if all goes as planned, will move out one day. Without looking back. You live for them, but you're building them for a world without you. Perhaps to be a father one day. A father who will learn that being a dad is never not having something in your hands and two thoughts in your head. One of those thoughts always being "I love kid."

# Keep Yourself Alive

"If it weren't for rock music, I'd be dead."

I realized it was one of the things that separated me from "them:" I listened to Slade, Deep Purple and Mott the Hoople. Soon there'd be T. Rex, the Sex Pistols and the Buzzcocks.

My best friend when I was fifteen was even littler than me. We were joined at our tiny hips. We weren't unpopular; we were just *not* popular. There is a big difference, as we would often discuss. We had plenty of time on our hands for such discussions. People didn't dislike us; they just didn't notice us. But I would calm my Little Friend by telling him that the world was run by people who were not popular in high school. So obviously, our futures were quite bright.

We wandered around, waiting for the world that we had such disdain for to notice us. We were like an old married couple. We didn't have kids, but we did have a record collection. We shared a record collection. See, neither of us had the money to buy a whole disc every week, so we'd split it.

Every Friday, we'd go into Sound Scapes, run by Barry. Barry was an artist in the way he'd pull out a record and look at it in the light, blowing off imaginary dust. He was an old guy, almost thirty, who was even more obsessed with music than we were. He told me once that he had chosen music over his marriage. Even as a teenager, I knew that there was probably more to the story than that.

Under his guidance, we'd buy our "treat of the week." This was the old days, when you could walk into a record store and know every record in there. And we did. Now it's like trying to memorize the faces of everyone in Manhattan. So many— similar, yet different.

This Friday, there was a record we'd never seen before. It was red. It was mysterious. It was Queen.

Barry said, "Want to partake?"

Of course we did. He took his pointy, divorced thumbnail and slid it across the cellophane seam. Such a beautiful sensation; even now, it sends shivers through me. He put it on. "Keep Yourself Alive" leapt from the turntable. That weird, spacey rock guitar started coming at us. Frightening, yet so comforting. If you have access to it, go play it right now. I'll wait . . .

Am I right? Isn't it fantastic? It blew our young rock minds. We pulled out our money, but Barry stopped us.

"You've been in here every Friday for a year and a half. Every so often, you buy something stupid that I don't understand, like the Turtles." My Little Friend looked down sheepishly at his platform shoes.

"But you've understood the things I've played for you. Mountain, Uriah Heep and yes, even Hawkwind. You guys have good taste." We were almost crying by now.

"So I'm gonna give you this record for free."

That's when we started to cry. It was Friday night, we had the greatest record we'd ever heard and our money was still in our white pants pockets.

Outside, a Vega GT full of cowboy assholes raced past us screaming, "Losers!" A cowboy in the car flicked a lit cigarillo at our heads. "Wine-flavoured and honey-dipped," as the ads boasted. The cigarillo bounced off my chest into the snow. As my head bowed in defeat, I saw an ember of hope. The burning cigarillo had landed in the snow. It was almost perfectly good—only two drags had been taken. So I picked it up, butted it out and smiled at my Little Friend. We had the world's greatest record. We had a cigar. This was no regular Friday. We needed to see where this night was headed. Meaning, try to get some beer.

So we hitchhiked to Woolco—or, more importantly, to the liquor store next to it. We were only fifteen, but "hauling out" is a great noble Canadian tradition. One guy helping out another. Sort of like boosting your car, except perhaps it's technically illegal. We found our man, telling him, "We have to celebrate something very special," which was sort of true. He agreed to go in for us. Awesome. Or "copacetic," as we said in those days. We hummed "Keep Yourself Alive" as we waited excitedly by the snowbank.

A minute later, this gentleman, this angel in a jean jacket, came out with some beer. Molson Golden. A cheap beer that they have since stopped making because of the taste.

As we took the beer, we realized there was a flaw in our plan. The plan had no phase two. How were we going get the case back to our neighbourhood? My Little Friend attempted to cover it with his satin bolero jacket, but it was too small. Worried, I told him not to worry.

I walked into Woolco, thinking, "It's not a crime to steal bags because they don't actually charge for them. It's only a crime if you shoplift the things that would go into those bags."

I whistled, trying to be inconspicuous, thus drawing attention to myself. I breezed up to an empty cash register and grabbed some bags. But as I turned, there stood a woman who said, "Yes? Can I help you with something?

I spun. "Um, it's good you caught me. My dad wants me to get a bag. He's really stupid," which was partially correct. She glared at me.

"Our dog is really sick."

This made little sense to her, but still, she let me have a huge red and white Woolco bag. Yes! It was a night filled with grace. We had the greatest record of all time, a cigarillo, a case of beer and now, a way to conceal it.

Outside, we wrapped the beer in the bag. We stood by the busy road, attempting to hitchhike home. Almost immediately, a Sincere Professor in his little MG pulled up.

He asked, "What's in the bag?"

I replied with the first thing that came to mind, "An Apache tent, sir." I'm not really sure what an Apache tent is, but he bought it.

"You're the outdoor type. Just like my son. Hop in."

As we drove, he explained that his son had recently borrowed his car, and afterwards the Professor had found a hash pipe under his seat. He confronted his son, who told him it wasn't his, and the Professor believed him. In fact, he was going to the police station to turn it in, but he was already late to meet some people for cheesecake. (This was something that actually happened in Alberta in the eighties. Groups of eight or ten would go out and just eat cheesecake. It was a puzzling phenomenon indeed.)

The Professor opened the glove box and showed us the hash pipe. We pretended that is was scary to us, which it wasn't.

Then, in a moment of youthful bravado, I said, "You know, my dad's a cop." Which, of course, was bullshit. "I can give it to him if you want."

Touched by my helpfulness, the Professor smiled.

The trusting fool wrapped the pipe in a paper towel and handed it to me, saying, "You're just like my son."

I thought, "Yes, we are. And now we have his hash pipe." We drove into the perfect night, our "Apache tent" rattling away in the back.

We walked through our townhouse community, Brae Glen, looking for a party. And we found one!

Our plan was simple: go in, chug some warm beer, smoke a cigar, pass around our new hash pipe and play the world's greatest record that we just happened to have. And in so doing, we would become heroes.

As we entered, there was a beautiful girl wearing baby-blue eye shadow, a velvet choker with a cameo on it and fur-fringed leather jacket. You know the type. She was stunning and perhaps six months older than me. But on a night like this, I thought she might fall in love with me. She put her Frye boot in front of me, stopping our entry. "Yes?" she said.

What to do? I opened the paper towel, revealing the hash pipe. She smiled and took it, letting us pass.

We located the record player, which had some bullshit blaring from it. Probably Cat Stevens's *Tea for the Tillerman* or Elton John's *Madman Across the Water*. Or *Homecoming* by America, the worst of the lot. This was it. I scratched the record off for effect. And may I just say that this was years before they did this in every bad movie trailer. I scratched the record off and turned to the now-stunned party.

"We are musical geniuses. We're ahead of our time. It's almost like we're from the future! We are going to play a record that will change this party and your lives forever."

I slid the needle over and put on Queen. The guitar started to riff.

"Perfect," I thought, "it's happening." But as I looked back, they were not transformed. I noticed a sea of unimpressed faces. A sea that turned rough.

Then, from the kitchen, where all the hot-knifing had been taking place, came the guys from the Vega GT. The biggest one asked me what the fuck I thought I was doing.

My terror-filled answer was, "Don't bother me! I'm in the belly of the beast."

I don't know why I said that. I just said it. Perhaps the beast I was referring to was the music. Although, as I think about it, "Don't bother me, I'm in the belly of the beast" is a pretty good response in almost any situation.

Someone is arguing with you over a parking spot? "Don't bother me, I'm in the belly of the beast."

"Honey, who was that redhead I heard you were with?"

"Don't bother me! I'm in the belly of the beast."

Okay . . . it may not work in every situation.

Then the Jumbo Cowboy yelled, "Gay fags!" I pointed out that "gay" and "fags" are the same thing. Shouldn't he just scream one or the other? Wouldn't that be more efficient? Or how about "short fags," or even "stupid fags," as others had done? But there we stood, "gay fags." He was not impressed. He leaned in, ready to punch my face.

My sense of humour's gotten me out of trouble. But more often, it's almost gotten me killed. Like on this night. I was a big Bugs Bunny fan at the time—moreover, a Daffy Duck fan. And I sort of resembled Daffy Duck in a short leather jacket and wide-legged jeans. So I waited for him to call me a fag again, and when he did . . . I kissed him. I kissed him right on his tobacco-scented lips and said, "What's up, Doc?" Like I believe Bugs Bunny had once done. He reached out to kill me, and we ran.

We made it outside and heard the music majestically still blaring. We looked at each other like we were the coolest guys in the world.

Then the music stopped; the record was thrown out the front door into the snow. We grabbed it just before the freshly kissed Cowboy could catch us. We darted out into the perfect Friday night.

Three blocks later, we slowed down. I lit the cigarillo and passed it to my Little Friend. We smoked it victoriously. Because we were no longer not popular. We were now unpopular.

# Punk History

If it weren't for ketchup, I'd be dead. It's all I ate growing up. I was raised in the West, where ketchup was king. When I was a kid, I didn't know vegetables even existed. As a teenager, I saw a kiwi and ran screaming from the store. I was shown a pineapple on my twenty-first birthday in a gentleman's club. I remember the summer that guacamole came to town. Children held the hands of their parents and waited patiently just to catch a glimpse of it. Old people wanted no part of it, turning back to their divining rods and butter churns.

It's too bad that the great private journey of growing up has to happen in public. It's too bad that the complicated act of becoming one's self looks so ungainly from afar. We all know that we are different. But at first, we have no idea in what way. I've always felt like an outsider. Which is perhaps a fancy word for "loser." But I think I would rather be a loser than a "winner." As I have learned in my lucky life: outsiders, there sure are a lot of us. At first, just enough to fill a rusty Toyota Corolla that doubled in value every time we filled it up with gas. Later, enough to make up a comedy troupe.

Back then, most of the guys had their cars up on blocks. They kept their cars on pedestals, but not their women. I have a small scar on my lip from stopping a guy from hitting his wife in a Mac's Milk. She gave it to me, not him. I was supposed to be minding my own F'n' business, apparently.

I didn't know what I wanted to be; I only knew what I didn't want to be. I didn't want to be like "them"—society. Whatever *that* was. I didn't want to be like the jocks with the blow-dried hair. Or worse, the cowboys. The guys driving around in trucks blaring the Irish Rovers or, at best, Three Dog Night.

You were considered gay if you kept your change in your wallet. Or had manners.

Cowboys chased me, offended that I wore a pink T-shirt. If you wore one, you were considered gay. I wasn't gay. But if I had been, it would've made sense. 'Cause then I'd know why I wasn't like them.

The cowboys didn't like that I wore pyjamas with two tartan neckties. Or a cravat, with a sleeves-torn-off Boy Scout shirt tucked into cranberry-coloured jeans. Jeans tucked into ratty white go-go boots. I also wore nurse's shoes to rankle them, and somewhat for the comfort.

As a young man, I didn't know what I was doing with my life. I had no idea. All I had was my sense of humour, and *that* kept me going.

People always say humour helps to avoid the dark things in life. I think it's the opposite. Humour helps us understand and partner with the sadness and beauty of life. And sometimes, because we're bathed in laughter, we are protected. Or at least, humour can help us see the world differently.

I remember walking through a thrift store, at sixteen, looking through old, weird books. I searched religiously, but not for religion. I wasn't sure what I was looking for. My sense of humour feels like it was formed almost entirely in this instant; I opened an old sixth-grade health book. Inside was a drawing of a "Sloppy Boy" with his hair askew, and beside him, a "Good Boy" with his hair combed, smiling. The caption read, "It's important to be well groomed." But out of the Good Boy's head, some like-minded vandal had drawn an arching, spurting dink.

I thought, "Yes, this is what *those* people look like to us." I was alone, but I laughed. Knowing I was not alone.

In a couple of years, I would grab a tartan notebook and start writing things down. Anything I thought was funny, weird or just needed to be written down. But until I began posing as a writer, the thing I had to protect me was music. It's what I did. I latched onto anything loud, odd and from far away. When I heard the English punk group Gang of Four sing "At Home He's a Tourist," I was sure they knew me, somehow.

Me and my Little Friend would sit for hours, doing nothing but listening to music. Sometimes we would read liner notes, or drum on our knees. But then we would go back to pure, uninterrupted listening.

No one has more time on his hands than an unpopular sixteen-year-old boy. We went to any rock concert in town. Especially if the bands came from somewhere else. Like England. Wow. We'd hold on to the front door of the Calgary Corral at noon. Then, around six, they would open the door and we (and only we) would sprint to the front of the stage. And wait two or three hours till the show started.

We were there once to see Joe Cocker. He had come to town for some quick change. He had a look that said, "What shit town have I found myself drunk in this evening?" When he sang, "Not feeling too good myself," I believed him. And—I will never forget this—on his monitor, beside his set list, was another piece of paper. One he could see and, presumably, we could not. In roadie-scrawled handwriting, the paper said "Calgary." To remind the world-weary musician where this stopover gig was: "Joe, you are in Calgary." And between songs, whenever he glanced down and thanked "Calgary," I thought it was hilarious.

After the show, I stole that paper from the monitors. Jumped partway up on stage and grabbed it before I could be repri-manded (get my head kicked in). I stuck it on my wall beside my Uriah Heep and Wishbone Ash posters.

"Calgary. Tonight, Bruce, you have found yourself in Calgary." But not for long. I knew I would someday be leaving.

It became my job to leave town. Me and my Little Friend talked about it constantly. Would we go to Vancouver, where the girls were "easier"? Or go to Toronto, where there was a better music scene? Or perhaps even Montreal, where it was rumoured you could get an apartment with a fireplace for a hundred dollars a month. I never found out. I would eventually choose Toronto.

Calgary is now a place where oilmen fight nightly for tables in wine bars. When I was growing up, there were no wine bars. Only bars. The Shamrock, the Calgarian, the Port O'Call Inn. A port in the storm and a good place to get your ass kicked. You'd receive a beating for half price between three and six. "Happy hour," I believe they called it.

I confess that, as a younger man, I drank in places so backward that they thought *Hee Haw* was a documentary. I drank in places so low-end that they'd chain the toilet paper up in the bathroom. And the other guys who drank there couldn't seem to figure out how to steal it. (You unrolled it back onto a new loop you created. Hey, I was broke.)

I confess that I did, on occasion, get so drunk that the only food I could ever eat again was bacon. And the only thought I could ever think again was "bacon."

I have gotten so drunk, I had to call in sick, only to be told, "You don't work here." And realized that I'd just driven by the place the night before and kind of mixed everything up. And when they asked who I was, said the only thing that seemed to make sense: "Bacon . . . I'm Bacon Boy?"

We drank at the Calgarian Hotel. First, we took the Natives' land, then we took their bar. And if you were in the Calgarian around last call, I think there was actually an announcement that said, "Pair up and fight now." You'd get grabbed. Someone twice as big as you would look over and say, "What's your problem?"

"I don't have a problem. What's *your* problem?"

"My problem is that you don't have a problem."

So you would "go." You'd find yourself outside surrounded by men chanting, "Fight, fight, squish his F'n' eye, squish his F'n' eye!" He would, and you'd see oblong for weeks.

I've had the same haircut practically all my life. Short back and sides, and just enough left on top not to be suspect. I did change my hair once: I varied the part to punish society. I started combing it on the other side. I thought, "I'll show you, society. Because you produce people lacking in the courage to take a leap to be different, I'm going to wear my hair on a slightly less flattering side."

I was a punk. It wasn't obvious, but if you asked me, I'd tell you—unless I swore at you, being a punk and all. Being a punk rocker in the early eighties was easy. You just slept in one day and you were labelled.

"Mom, did you notice your little boy's hair? I have something in it called gel. And human spit—not all of it mine. I'm here to announce that I'm not going to live in your microwave-oven world any longer. Don't heat up the Velveeta, Mom. Why don't you try heating up your own cold life? See, I'm not into your institutions anymore, like 'breakfast.' It's not the most important meal of *my* day, old lady. I'll have my eggs when I want and the way I want. And I don't want my eggs over easy. I want my eggs with the pain of the common man. Eggs Kerouac. And Mom, could you please fuck off while you bake?"

It was worse with my dad.

"Bruce, you and these new friends are out of control. You do everything Terry Shinky tells you to do. If Terry Shinky jumped off a bridge into a river, would you?"

"Of course. Terry and I have a suicide pact . . ."

As a young man, I fought the world hard. I had my fists in the air. My dad taught me to be strong by being weak. My mom taught me love by not loving me. My sister taught me to "follow your dreams" by getting a series of wage-slave jobs. I've had to work for minimum wage, and the worst thing about minimum wage isn't the money; it's the people. The other guys you have to work with. Guys named Leon. Guys who have their names tattooed on their arms for quick reference.

I worked at Canada Dry. The entire job interview was, "Do you mind getting wet?"

"Nope."

I got the job. I had to wear a uniform, but the name I wore on my shirt was Ricky. It drove the other guys crazy.

"I know for a fact that your name is not Ricky."

"No, but perhaps Ricky is the name of the shirt?"

I'd ride around in trucks with these guys, constantly writing things down in my little tartan notebooks. It made them nervous. As if it was, "Leon hears his name. Checks his arm. Then answers."

I told them I was a writer, even though I wasn't yet. But I read the *New Yorker*. I coveted it like it was porn. When no one was looking, I would glance at it. Devour it. Memorize the pages. The "About Town" tidbits. I knew then that one day I would be leaving.

One time, I went in to work at Canada Dry after a particularly long night. The route boss told me I would be driving a load of pop to Drumheller. An overnight trip to Drumheller. I said no. He asked me why. I answered, "'Cause I'm a genius." It came from inside. It was the only time in my life that I truly felt like one. I ranted on about how "no one should ever go to Drumheller. It's useless and lonely."

In the end, I didn't take the overnight trip, or quit, or even get fired. I would wear my green uniform, my Ricky shirt, on and off for the next two years. Proving, of course, I was far from a genius.

Many years later, I finally did get to Drumheller. My wife and I drove through it on an ill-planned road trip. And as the dusty wind bustled through our rented car, I realized that, even though I had been a young asshole, I was sometimes right. No one should ever go to Drumheller.

# Tequila-Fest

"The year you want to forget, you never do."

As any waiter who's had to put up with me can attest, I have abandonment issues.

"Where have you been?" I will ask.

"Do you need more coffee? The bill?"

"No, just some attention. Frankly, I wasn't sure if you were even coming back."

Here's why: my mom left when I was young.

My dad used to say to her, "What happened to the girl I married?"

And I'd think, "Well, she had to watch *you* all these years, Dad."

Growing up in our weird version of a family, my mom eventually became quiet and withdrew. Then she withdrew all the money from my parents' bank account and took off with "some white-haired lunk." Family lore. So short and swift in the retelling. But there was also the slamming of car doors. Swearing through screen doors. Tears in the shepherd's pie. The usual. So I come from a broken home. A setback which I think the optimists of today call "an opportunity."

There were only two channels on TV back then. So it was quite entertaining to the neighbours when my parents would fight in front of our house. As people nowadays say on Dr. Phil, "We fight all the time. But never in front of the children." Back then, it seemed normal to fight in front of the children while blowing smoke rings around their heads and telling them it was their fault.

I remember my dad grabbing Mom by the hair once. Luckily, it was around the time when wigs were becoming popular. So the red pelt that my mom wore just came off in his hand, revealing a matted field of confused grey hair. Presto! Like some grim magic trick. But still I have to agree with all the neighbourhood children who laughed. It was somehow quite funny. I guess you had to be there. And, yes, *I* had to be.

A couple of years later, she and the lunk broke up. Mom moved out on her own. A free woman for the first time in her life, in her forties. She began selling real estate. The great rebound career of so many. She did well and lured me to move in with her. I moved into her rec room. Which I would later wreck.

It was the last year of high school. Happy times at first. I began running hard. Lifting weights. I wandered into a club where weights clanged and coaches coached. I started doing the snatch and the clean and jerk. And competing. My nickname at the time became "Power Jerk," and I think both parts were true.

One day, while being weighed for a competition, I had a great (terrible) idea: "Tequila-Fest." Even though none of us had ever drunk tequila, Tequila-Fest would be a competitive drinking event for me and my semi-circle of friends. A competitive drinking event for high school students—how badly can that end?

I made up fliers and rules. What would a competitive drinking event with a bunch of teenagers be without rules?

My friends came over to my house. Well, my mom's house. Although, in truth, it would soon belong to the bank.

My mom and her "suitor of the week," as I called them, went out for the night. She was planning to stay out late, so we could have the ruin of the place. I mean, *run* of the place. I'm getting ahead of myself.

It was their first date, but she would end up in his arms. This was the old days. If you wanted to woo a woman, you'd wine and dine her. At that time, it was all surf 'n' turf: buttery lobster, beef, wine and, for dessert, Bailey's, mud pie and menthol cigarettes. I'm foreshadowing.

At my mom's house, my friends and I stripped down to our little Adidas running shorts and had the "weigh-in." Possibly a little homoerotic, in retrospect, but it's what we did. We weighed ourselves to see how much tequila per pound we could drink.

Once we were all ready, I rang a bell I'd found in a box marked "Christmas" and declared, "Gentlemen, start your drinking." With that, we commenced the "Welcome, Warmup Shots" as outlined in the program. What I had imagined as an elegant round-robin quickly turned to ratshit. Things devolved from there. I don't think we ever figured out who won, or even awarded the bowling trophies I had gotten from the thrift store as prizes.

We totalled my mom's house. She came home later that night and found me on the lawn. I was lying on it in a state of repose. Well, more specifically, in the fetal position. Asleep. Wearing only Adidas shorts, wrapped in silly string. The silly string had matted and melted because I'd thrown up inside the cocoon it had made. The string was supposed to be for when we announced the winner. But, of course, there were no winners.

As Mom went inside, first the smell, and then the carnage, greeted her. Various tableaus of debauchery: a tequila bottle in the fish tank, shoes floating in an overflowing bathtub, lipstick drawn on her *Blue Boy* painting. Everything, everywhere had been smashed. We had broken every glass but one: a pewter mug that we had only dented.

My mother took one look, wobbled out and had a heart attack. That's how she ended up in the arms of her suitor. He got her into bed. Too bad for him, it was a hospital bed.

My older sister rushed to the hospital and took charge. The doctor told us our mom was now stable. She had a major blockage, so it would have happened sooner or later anyway. After he left, my sister turned to me. "Don't blame yourself."

"Good," I said.

"No, blame yourself *and* your friends."

There would be no Tequila-Fest II.

Mom fell on tough times. She couldn't work, so the bank took the house. She moved into an apartment with my sister, and I was not invited. I was essentially homeless. I realized then that we are all merely three bad breaks away from living in a cardboard fort. But writing that down in my little tartan notebook didn't make my life any easier.

I was, for the first time in my life, on my own.

There was no music that year. Figuratively and literally. The stereo I was given as a graduation gift had to be taken back. My once-generous mom needed to get her hands on any cash she could. No, there was no music that year, only the sounds of machines and the buses I took to get to various wage-slave jobs.

I began my lost year. I was like a pinball, slamming through life. Attracted to things that would only repel me. I was lost, so I said yes to whatever jobs came my way. I did roofing in the middle of winter. I fell off a lot. The guy I was working for said, "If only you were as good at building roofs as falling off of them." Then I constructed metal barns in the middle of summer under the tutelage of a cruel German. He wouldn't let me off the top of the barn at lunch. He'd just throw a sandwich up to me and I'd gobble it like the thankful animal I'd become.

Then I sold Ginsu knives door to door. I mean, I *tried* to sell them. At one of the first houses I went to, a greasy guy took all the sample knives, went inside and locked the door.

Next, I handed out fliers, but got caught putting a thousand into a mailbox.

I would go to the bus station and say to the person working at the lost and found, "I lost my sweater." Then they'd pull out a box. I'd see any sweater and go, "Yeah, that one there. And oh, you found my watch," I would add as I picked out a women's watch. "Fantastic!" I'd end up with most of the box to sell or trade. I was broke.

I would wait outside the bakery for the donuts to turn day-old so I could get them cheaper. Now what was I supposed to do? I had tried everything I could think of. Nothing was working. I felt so lost. I felt so old. I was twenty. Even as someone who wasn't quite a writer yet, I knew this that was a low point.

At least I hoped it was a low point.

I would soon get an idea to get me out of the hole I was in, but it would leave me somewhere even worse.

# Under the Rug

"Ever get up and go somewhere and not know why you went there?

That happened to me. I went to college."

I did what countless lost souls had done before me: I went to college.

I took business for some reason. Perhaps a practical joke I was playing on myself. There are a few things in my life it feels like I've watched myself do, if you know what I mean. Taking business at Mount Royal Community College was one of them.

I had a girlfriend who was in the business program with me. She went in and picked up our grades. She said, "Between us, we got 100 per cent." I thought, "50/50? Not too shabby. Or

60/40? I can dig out from under a 40." No, she got 80 per cent, I got 20. In truth, I don't think I deserved that much. So sad when even the compromise you make in your life to sell out doesn't work out.

One night, I went to see Theatresports by mistake. I thought it was something like Reveen the Impossibilist, the hypnotist who used his piercing eyes and stacked-up pompadour to ferret out your secrets. I was young then. My secrets were few. So I went.

But Theatresports was even scarier than Reveen. It was comedy improv. Competitive and cruel. Exhilarating.

Onstage, there they stood, the small-world legends. Day jobbers by day, improvisers by night. They were the coolest people I had ever seen. Perhaps they still are. They performed with nothing in their hands or their heads. The audience threw "boo-bricks" at them when, or if, they failed. Even crueller, the judges held up numbers to grade the scenes and would stop them in mid-stream if they sucked. The improvisers didn't care. Failure was their whiskey. I later learned that bourbon was also their whiskey.

I stared up at that stage. I'd found my place. Even though I had no idea how to get up there.

I walked up to someone after the show. How silly I suddenly felt in my "creative clothes"; cowboy shirt, two paisley scarves, painter pants and wrestling boots covered in wood-grain Mactac. They told me to enrol in classes. I did. There, I met Theatresports founder Keith Johnstone. He was not from there. He was from somewhere else. You could tell by the way he wore Ski-Doo boots well into June. He embraced me and all the other outsiders who straggled in. He taught me to "just make things up. Try to not be boring. But don't try to be interesting, either. That can be a lot worse."

I stopped dressing creatively, because I was finally being creative. I began wearing a grey T-shirt and army pants—camouflage, because I didn't want to stand out anymore. I wanted to blend in. And do something.

I leapt up the stairs each night to go to my class. Afterwards, I'd lie in bed, my heart pounding, thinking about everything I had said and done in class.

One day, they told me I was getting to do a show. A live show. A ten-minute Theatresports game for an audience.

The big night, I sat at the side of the stage, cotton-mouthed and clammy, my fists hiding in the pockets of my army pants. It was excruciating as I waited to get up onstage. Eight minutes into the ten-minute game, I still hadn't gotten on. I thought, "Oh well, I can go be a welder or something." Thinking that if I had to wait another week, it was all over for me. That's how precarious my future felt. Finally, someone tapped me on the forearm. I was going to be in the next scene.

It was called "the hat game." The game was simple: you and your scene partner put on hats and the goal was to steal the other person's hat. Using the first rule of improv—never say no—you could finagle your partner into a position perfect for plucking.

"Help me change this tire. That's right, bend down . . ." And *bam*, you'd grab his hat.

But probably he'd say, "I'll change the tire . . . if you kiss it first."

And on it would go. I hated the hat game.

I stood up, put my hat on, but was struck by the idea that it would be funny if I went under the rug.

There was a large rug that covered the stage. I bellowed over to my bewildered scene partner, "I'm gonna dig a tunnel," and down I went. Beneath the heavy, hot smelly rug. I couldn't see. And I could barely hear. After a minute or so, I heard angels singing. I mean, the sound of laughter, which is sort of the same thing. A beautiful sound. Sometimes elusive. Always welcome.

Trouble was, I had another fifty feet of rug to go. By the time I crawled out the other side, there stood my scene partner.

"Here, kind sir, please take my hat," and I handed it to him.

He couldn't say no. All three judges threw up zeros. I felt the soft pelting of boo-bricks that I would soon become accustomed to. It feels like, for the rest of my creative career, I have been going under the rug, doing things that please the few, and not the many. The only person who thought it was funny that night was Mark McKinney.

We quickly became complicated friends as we melded our comedy brains together. We tried writing. I opened up my tartan notebook, hoping I finally had a place for these tidbits.

"Arms won't bend. It's a scene about a guy whose arms won't bend."

Mark would consider this like a scientist, then give his findings: "It's funny because he can't do push-ups. Next."

"I also have an idea for a song called 'The Daves I Know.' It's a list of all the guys I know named Dave."

"Or perhaps named David?" offered Mark.

Then I'd say, "Naked for Jesus. It's a good title, but I don't know what the scene is."

"Obviously, we'd have to be naked."

Then, like a gunslinger, Mark pulled out his tidier black book and read, "'Woodstock puppet show.' We act out the whole concert in two minutes."

I groaned inside because that was such a good idea. Why hadn't I thought of it? But still, I made a cardboard Jimi and Janis for his scene and he'd eventually strip down to be naked in mine.

We begged Theatresports to let us perform some of these scenes after the shows, and unbelievably, they let us. It sort of worked. People stayed and laughed. Then there was a tipping point, where people started to show up just to see us and forgo Theatresports. We were young and selfish then, so we didn't understand why that wasn't a lot of fun for the Theatresports players.

Mark, a few others and I would do anything we thought was funny. Or better yet, weird. One time before a show, we holed up in the men's bathroom with an electric bass and drums, waiting. We liked the idea that, as soon as someone came in, we'd start playing and sing about whatever we saw, "Man in leather jacket walks into bathroom. Look how hastily he unzips his fly." But it didn't work too well because a guy would walk in, see two preening nerds with a bass and drums and leave.

So then we moved ourselves into a stall. It was a tight fit, but I was so skinny back then, I could fit through a dog door (and I'd often have to when the "other boyfriend" came home). So we crammed ourselves into the stall, and as soon as we heard someone start to pee, we'd start to play. This worked better, because when a guy starts to pee, he usually doesn't stop till he's done.

After three or four of these urinal concerts, there was a banging on the stall door. We opened it, and there stood a cop. Suddenly, it hit me that what we were doing might be illegal. Being in a bathroom and singing about people peeing could be against the law. He said no, we weren't being charged with anything. In fact, he thought what we were doing was sort of funny. (Yes, he said "sort of." I always remember the "sort of" part.) He gave us his card and told us if we wanted to make some money, he might be able to get us a gig.

Then he slipped into the stall next to us. We didn't know what to do. After he "began," we couldn't help ourselves. "Shitting cop just gave us his card. Now he hit the toilet. He's hitting it hard . . ."

# Prison Break

I had just gotten off the phone. It was a tough negotiation. I'd told him that Steve Martin got $25,000 a show. He didn't care. We were stuck at his original offer. So I took it.

I walked into rehearsal to tell Mark and the other four that we had gotten a big, fat paying gig. "Two hundred dollars." Their mouths fell open. Mark, a human abacus, computed, "That's $33.33 each." The guys were ecstatic. Then they asked where this gig was. I was evasive, and for good reason. "Out of town," I told them. "Hey, can we stop asking dumb questions and rehearse?"

"Where exactly is this show?"

"It's in a prison," I replied nonchalantly. They laughed until they realized I was telling the truth. Mark wondered, "Do prisons have theatres?"

"No, we're in the commissary. Or maybe they call it a mess hall." Then we tried to decide what stuff we would perform. I said, "Let's do all our prison material." We quickly realized: we had no prison material.

So we desperately tried to rewrite stuff we had done to fit. Mark: "Can't one of the Daves you know be a guy who's up for parole?"

"For sure, let's not play bass and drums when they walk into the bathroom."

We joked about all the things we would try: an improv game where we'd carve things out of soap. We'd make up a song about their trials. But we were concerned that nothing rhymed with "guilty." Nothing seemed to click.

We were all trying to control our panic. I think Mark started babbling, "Thirty-three thirty-three, thirty-three thirty-three," to calm himself. I was worried.

Back then, it felt like any setback could mean the end of us. We were like a fragile couple who could break up if they didn't agree on what to order on a pizza.

The six of us crammed into my Toyota Corolla and made our way towards the penitentiary. But as we pulled up to the checkpoint, things stopped being funny real fast. There was the rigmarole of serious security and paperwork. As the guards searched our costumes and props, we realized how flimsy and gay we seemed. The guard said, "You guys don't seem very funny." For some reason, I blurted, "We are the funniest stars under heaven."

He just stared at me. "They're going to eat you alive."

As I gathered my props to walk in, the guard grabbed my arm. "Whatever you do, don't ask them what they're in for."

Backstage, I peered through the makeshift curtain and saw a frightening parade. In marched three hundred prisoners who hadn't beaten anyone up in a while. It was a sea of folded, tattooed arms.

First up was an improv, and I had to warm up the crowd. I pranced out, trying not to prance. I started to warble, my nervous voice suddenly higher than a nightingale's, and I turned to a guy in the front row who looked like Charles Manson without the charisma.

"What are you in for?"

I said it was the guard's fault for planting that seed in my impressionable brain.

He stared at me for about a minute, then said, "Assault."

Then I spit out the first thing that came into my head, and you know how dangerous that can be. I actually said, "Then the guy sitting next to you must be in for 'a-pepper.'" Salt and pepper.

It took even me, the man who had blurted out this terrible children's joke, a minute to get it. The cruel coincidence was that "Salt" was white, and "Pepper," of course, was black. A weird you-may-get-killed-soon laugh rolled up from the mess hall. In the wings, the warden starting barking orders into his walkie-talkie. Riot prep, I presume.

With the crowd now "warm," I asked for a suggestion. "May I please have a location?"

A voiced boomed out, "Rape cage."

I gulped. "I believe the first thing I heard was . . . laundromat."

I looked at Mark. It was going to be a long show. After a mime piece in a laundromat, I went into some of my "killer standup."

"Wow, things are pretty weird on TV these days. Like that commercial for Charmin. Do you know what that is? Do they let you guys watch TV?" Blank stares.

"Do they let you have toilet paper?"

It was not good. Then I made the critical error of trying to relate to them. "Man, I bet things don't make sense in here, but it's even crazier out there."

*Out there?* Bruce, quit reminding them that they're incarcerated!

"Out there, you go shopping . . . how come hot dogs come in packs of eight, but buns come in packs of twelve? Are they trying to fuck with us?" I said "fuck," trying to express the anger they must have felt. "No Bruce," I thought, "do universal stuff."

"You know when you break up with your girlfriend? How you find yourself listening to Air Supply and thinking, 'This music is so true?'" I realized that when these men broke up with their girlfriends, they didn't go listen to the music of Air Supply. Perhaps that's what they were in for.

Next, Mark anchored a beat-poetry piece set to Johnny Cash's "Folsom Prison Blues." Which went over just as well as you imagine a beat-poetry piece about prison would go over . . . in a prison.

Not to worry. We still had our big finish.

In Calgary, we'd been closing our shows with a piece where we all wore women's swimsuits and bathing caps. We did a fully choreographed synchronized-swim routine set to "Dance of the Sugar Plum Fairy." It usually killed. But this was not our usual crowd.

I didn't understand much about sexuality or mob behaviour at the time, but when we scurried out in our girlfriends' bikinis, it became clear: we were in trouble. These guys hadn't seen anything that even represented a woman in a long time. I became conscious of all the skin I was showing. It was a lot, and at the time, I was young and supple. So I kind of resembled a woman—my fear had shrunken my manhood, and nerves had made my nipples hard.

When the show was on the verge of collapse, I launched into one of my patented, over-the-top nerd characters. I put on horn-rimmed glasses and pigeon-toed my feet, whining, "Hi, I'm the warden. You guys have no idea how hard my job is."

They cheered.

"If you don't make your beds, I'm going to pee myself and poop in my diaper. Yes, I have a big diaper under my pants. That's why my ass looks so fat."

I was getting juicy laughs. We somehow made it through the rest of the show.

I came offstage, and there stood the warden. "So you think I'm funny? Do you know why those guys didn't riot? Because they're afraid of me. You make fun of me in the next show, and I'll let them kill you."

Everything stopped. "The next show? We're doing *two* shows?"

The guys all turned to the man who had negotiated the deal: me. I had somehow misunderstood.

The warden explained that the second show was for the violent offenders. They needed their own because they couldn't be around the other prisoners.

"But they can be around us?" asked Mark.

Apparently, yes, they could. A glassy-eyed Mark started chanting "Thirty-three thirty-three, thirty-three thirty-three." But even that was of no comfort.

Then the warden explained, "You'll get paid for two shows."

"Sold!" said Mark, brightening.

Then the warden told us that, until showtime, we should wait in a "holding area." That had bars. Yes, a cell. So we sat in a cell, waiting for the brutality of failure to hit us again.

We made it through our second show. Believe it or not, it was worse than the first one. Afterwards, the warden walked us to the pay window. We would receive our payment in cash. We were confused when an employee asked us to sign for a giant stack of cash.

"Two hundred dollars. Per show. Each."

"Each?!" Mark exclaimed. "That's four hundred dollars. Each."

This paid better than every other gig we did for the next twenty years, and it was our first. Maybe we wouldn't be breaking up after all?

I turned to the warden: "Do you have any *really* violent offenders? Anyone on death row? You can easily hire us for one more show."

# The Last of One

When you're young, things happen in your life. At the time, they may seem like they will be the first of many, but often they're the last of one.

My first flush of success happened at the Edmonton Fringe Festival. I was performing my one-man show, *Trapped in a Lawn Chair*, with jokes that illuminated the human spirit like, "No, I wasn't masturbating in the bathtub. I was just cleaning it and it went off." *Boom*. Big laugh.

I was young, lucky and dumb in equal measure. People came, and even better, I was paid in cash. I was given fistfuls of two-dollar bills—yes, they existed back then—which I stuffed into the pockets of my Storm Rider jean jacket. Like "cash headlights," they lit my way as I went to celebrate my obvious success.

Since Tequila-Fest and the heart attack it inspired, my mom had had trouble finding work. She'd moved up to Edmonton for a job that fell through and was now scrambling to make ends meet. She was well known on the flea-market circuit. She'd go to garage sales, buy things, wash them and sell them as antiques. Garage-tiques, really. But it was almost an honest living. She also sold fire extinguishers out of the trunk of her car. I know this sounds like a joke, but it's true: she sold funeral plots door-to-door.

I always imagined she lugged the headstones, too. "Dad, why is there an old lady on our doorstep with a blank tombstone?"

They'd open the door and she'd point at it, saying, "Think about it: your loved one's name could go right here."

But the good news was she had just landed a rather plum job delivering pizzas.

She was quite excited to see me when I got to town for the festival. But I was now of the age where, maybe, I could squeeze her in if I had time. Your real independence doesn't happen when you storm out of your parents' house, your middle finger flapping in the wind. It happens when you come to town and don't call. But I would end up calling her because I had a job that was so crummy and low-paying that I couldn't think of anyone else to do it.

I drank bourbon back then. First for the idea, then for the taste. And, of course, because Daddy drank rye. I was quite sure I was nothing like Daddy. You're right, Bruce. He drank a lot of rye and you drank a lot of bourbon.

The only problem was that, this week, Alberta was locked in a bitter ALCB strike. The union that ran the liquor stores was locked out. The stores were not being restocked and were all almost empty. But I heard from a friend of a friend of a bartender that one location still had bourbon for sale. So the only way to get the bourbon young Mr. McCulloch required after his shows, to party with his "Fringe friends," was to cross a hostile picket line.

But I thought, "This isn't fair. Things come to me easily. All I should have to do is click the heels of my little cowboy boots that I wear ironically, and things should magically happen."

Enter Mom.

I had a nice habit of bringing up my mom's "one mistake" of abandoning me as often as possible, especially if I needed something. "Hey Mom, remember that time you put on a new wig and walked out?"

I went to see her and told her of my "bourbon problem." Using my improv skills, I spun a tale of the crazy demands that the lazy workers were making. Like extra money if they had to talk to customers, or if it was a windy day. Worse, they weren't even happy with the fifty bucks an hour they were already making! I had no actual information on what the workers made, or their demands, but I needed bourbon.

Then, I asked my mom if she would cross the picket lines for me. She took a drag on her menthol cigarette, in calm contemplation. Anger danced across her face. She butted out her Moore with her sandal and told me she was "amped" to go. She'd be happy to stick it to those "lazy, shit-for-brain bastards."

I handed Mom a pocketful of cash.

The union men turned from their placards as an old woman pushed past them. As she did, she shouted, "Money grubbers!" At this, I slunk down in her Dodge Dart, worried someone would recognize me. But also, I kind of hoped someone would recognize me. I *was* having some pretty good shows.

I kept the car running in case there was any real trouble. If there was, the plan was to take off, and Mom and I would "meet up later." My mom would be fine. She had survived Tequila-Fest. She was a bulldog.

I huddled down in the car and turned up the radio. "Patio Lanterns" by Kim Mitchell played. Actually, I can't be certain about this, but "Patio Lanterns" by Kim Mitchell always played in those days in Edmonton. Still does.

After a minute, the car door opened. I popped my head up from under the dashboard, where I was now hiding. It was my mom, empty-handed. "Brucie, I have a question. They're all out of the big bottles. Should I buy the little ones?"

"Yes Mom, get as many as your old arms can carry."

Moments later, she came out with about a hundred little airplane-sized bottles of Jack Daniels in her arms—apparently they had run out of bags. And in her hand was also a piece of paper. A job application. As it turns out, all the talk of what these "fat cats" were getting had made my mom to want to work there.

She sat in the car and filled out the application while the picketers circled the car. She moved through the confused picket line and into the store a third time to hand the application in. So much for the swift getaway.

Nights later, my hotel room and I were trashed. The floor was littered with tiny bottles, now empty, and three more shows' worth of cash. It was 2 a.m. "Some girl" and I had been partying (it actually said "Some Girl" on her driver's licence, I think). There was a knock at the door. It was the pizza we'd ordered. Some Girl opened the door, and there stood the pizza delivery person: my mom.

I guess this cheap hotel was on her route. I looked back over my shoulder, realizing we had put my tiny cowboy boots on the bedposts. I was shirtless. Some Girl was wearing even less. This picture was *not* a Mother's Day card.

My mom just stared and said, "Oh good Christ, Brucie."

I stammered awkwardly, "Well, good morning, little schoolgirl." Which I believe is a Chuck Berry song that I was quoting for no conceivable reason. My mom *tsk*ed at me and asked me to introduce my "friend." I couldn't. That would require a name.

A terrible moment, where Some Girl and my mom both realized I was hitting it pretty hard with a girl whose name I'd either never known or had forgotten.

So I gathered up all the cash on the floor and gave it to my mom, pretending that this was my plan all along. Like a funny surprise for her. Ha, ha? Disgusted, she handed Some Girl the pizza and left.

Afterwards, I felt sick and not successful at all. I knew it was the last time I would ever feel that ashamed.

But it wasn't. As it turned out, it wasn't the last of one. It was the first of many . . . I was young.

# *Food Repairman*

G etting a really good idea feels like a warm egg breaking inside your brain. As if God has smiled from above. But seeing as there is no God, I'll go with the egg thing.

Mark and me and a few others had moved to Toronto to be creative. All the time. Can you imagine how tiring that was? I'd draw cartoons, even though I couldn't draw.

I'd use fridge magnets, which were all the rage, to make freaky fridge-poems. When those ran dry, I'd type weird stories and poems loud and hard, trying to prove that writing was real work. Sometimes, we would just sit there and "be creative." Even less productive than you are envisioning.

Clearly, the women we knew back home had not made the journey with us. Just us guys. We were like the men on those gold-hunting TV shows. Except instead of saying "gold" all the time, we said "funny." We had come to town to "make it." Whatever that meant.

When we moved to Toronto, we even talked someone from the paper into writing a story about us. How we'd moved to town and we were going to "make it by repeating our success in Calgary." We actually said that. Both stupid and wrong. In Calgary, if people didn't like you, they would chase you down and pummel you. In Toronto, they just ignored you. Which was worse.

Toronto is a city that's cruel and dismissive—but in so many languages. So many cultures not to feel a part of.

We floundered for quite some time.

We'd meet for breakfast to get a good early start on being creative. Back then, you could get a seven-meat breakfast with three kinds of potatoes for a dollar.

We'd go to the Carlton Cinemas to heckle art movies. Laborious foreign films on suitcase-sized screens. But it didn't matter. Because they had cappuccino. Cappuccino in a movie theatre? This was a brave new world.

Bloor Street was littered with futon stores. You could buy a futon for seventy-nine dollars. Couch by day and bed by night. Uncomfortable by day and worse at night. But we didn't care. We had some "making it" to do.

Those futon stores eventually closed down and became vitamin stores. Those closed down and are now fro-yo shops. I wonder what they'll be in two years?

Luckily, we met Kevin McDonald and Dave Foley. They were young old men quoting vaudeville and Lenny Bruce. They wore overcoats year-round and quipped.

They were a breath of fresh air, always ready to laugh. Mark and I were more like boxers who knew when the other guy had landed a punch. Dave's witty in his sleep, even though he's a legendary insomniac. He didn't "technically" finish high school, so he made up for it by reading every book in the world. And Kevin was just happy to be there, talking and listening.

"Kevin, want to play Galaga?"

"No, but I'll watch. That could be fun."

But Kevin was funnier than anyone we had ever met. We had to try, but everything he did was effortlessly hilarious. Just standing there, he was funny. Watching him wait for the bus or read a menu was a comic event.

Dave and Kevin threw their lot in with Mark and me without question. Perhaps they were just too polite to say no. They were not the savages of the group. We were. With our ideas and plans.

Plans and goals. Oh, youth.

We rented theatres to put on our own shows. They were poorly attended despite the fact that I had postered till my back ached. We had a dumb rule, which I think I had insisted upon: never repeat material. So we would write new stuff every week. Perform it. No one would come. Then we would toss it away and do it all again the next week.

Nothing was working. Things were starting to fray. This was the first slump of our young careers. Kevin and Dave probably thought we were trying too hard. We thought we weren't trying hard enough.

"Come on, guys, let's repeat the success we had in Calgary!"

Kevin and Dave would stare at us, then quip about the *Hindenburg*.

One week, I had an idea. *The* idea. This was going to be a game-changer. The idea was that we should write a murder mystery (you're right, it's already bad) called "The Case of the Missing Donut." It features a reluctant, hard-boiled detective played by Dave, who solves the complicated case. "Reluctant" was Dave's twist. Perhaps reluctant because the material was so bad. The man can always spot a stinker.

In the scene, someone was strangling people with dental floss and taking their donuts! It was a disgruntled dentist. Obviously.

As if the sketch weren't bad enough, I had the added great (bad) idea that we should tape donuts under every seat to be revealed during the comic climax of the sketch.

"Every seat, Bruce?"

"Yes, every seat, Kevin!"

"Even though the last three shows, only five people came?"

"You heard me! Every seat! Anything (stupid) that's worth doing, is worth doing well."

So we taped up a hundred donuts under a hundred seats. I'd like to say in my own defence that this was well before Oprah started putting books and gifts under the audience's seats. It was a bad idea, but it *was* original.

So the idea totally failed. The six people who came saw the

donuts the moment they walked in. And they didn't wait for the comedy climax, as I had envisioned. They started throwing them from lights up. We were pelted. The stage became donut- and sugar-covered. So by the time Dave finally announced, "The donuts are hiding under our noses. Look beneath your boney bottoms," the audience was so far ahead of us that most of them had gone home. The one guy who took most of the donuts with him (and threw the rest the hardest) was Scott Thompson.

Having witnessed such a beautiful failure and seen the stubbornness to persevere that remained in us, Scott felt a kinship. He would be joining the troupe soon, but none of us knew it at the time. If he hadn't wandered in to see what all the fuss wasn't about, the Kids in the Hall would never have existed.

That week, I'd had another warm-brain idea at one of our "all the meats in the world" breakfasts. It was called "Food Repairman": a sketch about a working-class hero who travels around, repairing food. All the guys had raw enthusiasm for it. It had about three *Grapes of Wrath*–type speeches, but still, it was such a solid idea, we chose it to close the show. So even after the donut debacle, it worked. It shone through. People loved it.

The last few months had been a train wreck for us. We were almost out of the money we'd saved for the "big move." But we'd finally written a really good sketch. And for the first time, we decided to keep it and repeat it. A breakthrough.

I went home that night. Satisfied, I sat on my futon, thinking about how things were changing. I put on *Saturday Night Live*. One of the sketches that night was called "Food Repairman." It was about a working-class hero, going around, repairing food. I guess two writers had the same egg break in their heads in the same week. Or was it God? Obviously, there was no God. Or we wouldn't be starting from scratch. Again.

# The Bible

I read the Bible.

I highlight what's important.

I highlight the whole thing.

It really is a "good book."

I think there's more truth in here

Than in a phone book.

I think all of it is true,

Except the part that says,

"God exists."


I love that great old book.

It's funnier than a *Far Side* cartoon.

I like religion.

It gives dumb people something to do

That isn't scratching lottery tickets.

And when you think about it,

Reading the Bible,

Hoping you'll get into heaven,

And scratching lottery tickets

Are sort of the same thing.


I love religion.

Whenever I walk into a church,

All I ever tend to think is,

"What a great apartment this would make."


I read the Bible.

And in case you want to read it too,

I won't tell you how it ends.

Okay, I will.

You die.

# Crazy Chick Circa '86

I wake up in a haze. I wake, not with a start, but with a stop. As in stop, something's wrong. Something is very wrong. Lordy Gordy, Brucio, I think you've done it again.

I look over to the pillow beside me. There is a hair there that I don't recognize. It's not mine, that's for sure. It's a frizzy hair that has been dyed many, many times. Now it is so tough, you could pick a padlock with it.

I look down. On the Canada Dry crate that I keep my record collection in is a purple floppy hat. I own no purple floppy hat. On the floor is a fanny pack, clearly taken off in a hurry. In the air is the faint waft of vegan sweat and Sinutab. That's when I realize, "Yep, I did it again. I've gone home with a crazy chick."

I don't even want to talk about the shoes tucked under my bed—or should I say, futon. The heels of those shoes are worn to a grotesque angle. How could any shoes ever get worn to such an angle? From pacing? Circling? Circling the phone, waiting for a call that might never come? Being locked in an imbroglio with the Earthlink people?

Well, she got up early and helped herself to a few of my yellow Post-it notes. She's used them to put up affirmations on the wall:

"I deserve love."

"You deserve love."

"Please re-read the last two affirmations."

"Sign up for wok-cooking class."

My eyes turn onto this yellow-brick road of pain and reminder and follow it to the bathroom. She's in the bathroom right now, brushing her teeth and singing.

She's brushing her teeth using some weird recumbent tooth-brush that she pulled from her handmade purse. Wait, what is that song she's singing? Is that Eurythmics I hear? Or a mash up of The Smiths and Cocteau Twins? Oh no—it's the first lady of disappointment, Kate Bush.

Yep, buddy, that's what happens when you go home with the crazy ones.

Who am I kidding? I knew what I was doing. I saw her there, in the corner of the bistro, asking for more hot water for her cranberry tea.

I sauntered over and said, "Hey."

"Greetings," she offered.

She moved her bike helmet so I could sit down. I sat down. I asked what she was up to. She said, "Oh, just journalling."

"I dig chicks who journal. Journalling is the world's least marketable creative outlet."

She agreed "wholeheartedly." Then we talked. Or rather, *she* talked. I listened. I know how crazy chicks like guys who listen.

She told me about how the Inuit have eleven words for "depression," but only one for "spoon."

"You don't say?" I offered, without adding much.

I learned life had been hard for her, but that she had just turned a corner. Or she was just about to turn a corner. Or she had turned four corners and ended up back where she started from. Perhaps that would explain the shoes. She told me she made jewellery part time but was now thinking of starting a non-profit to make some money. Apparently, her landlord was breathing down her neck.

"I'd like to breathe down your neck," I said, as I flirtatiously tossed her a Ricola.

The next moves, I must admit, I've used before; I applied ChapStick to her parched lips and elbows. I ordered her a tofu martini. I waited patiently as she left a message on her answering machine for her cat to hear, telling him "Mommie is going to be home a little bit late . . ."

Back at my place, she put a pashmina over my lampshade and took off her three earrings. I knew from experience, it was *time*. I embraced her.

"Let's make you a little more comfortable," I said as I reached around and unclasped her fanny pack, muttering a playful "Oops . . . the wind." The fanny pack hit the floor with a satisfying thump.

We kissed hard. Noses bumped. We wordlessly negotiated where on each other's face our noses should go. Then, arms and legs intermingled; zippers and buttons were fumbled with. It seemed that as soon as she folded a garment, we were on to the next stage!

Then she stopped us for a moment, getting even more serious than before. She cracked her neck and announced that she didn't want to fuck me, but the man "I could become."

I thought, "Can't you just fuck the man I was?"

She rolled on a condom made of recycled materials. I think

it was hemp. It was bracing at first, but you got used to it. By recycling, she said, we could have sex not just for ourselves, but for the good of a dying planet.

"Sexy," I muttered.

Crazy chicks are loud in bed. That's one of the reasons we like them. She got on top of me and started flopping away. She screamed, "Make me forget him. Make me forget him!"

Of course, I wondered, "Forget *whom*?"

"You are not Santa! You are not my Santa. Tell me again there is no Santa! Tell me there's . . . no . . . Santa."

I had not played this specific game before. Or since. I have to admit, it was tough on me at the end; she was quite vigorous in her elliptical lurching. I was concerned, quite frankly, that my shaft could snap. The term "You break it, you bought it" even popped into my head.

After the lovemaking session was over, we lay in the darkness and looked up at the stars. Or where we thought the stars would be, through my ceiling. We shared our hopes and dreams. Me? I didn't have any. Hers involved finding a guy not like "the others."

"Maybe you?" she wondered.

Not a chance.

Then there was a long silence, like one you would hear on college radio. Neither of us knew what to say. My eyes drifted to the earring on the windowsill that, experience told me, she would probably forget. Finally, she offered, "Tomorrow? . . . I think you should drink a lot of water. People just don't drink enough water."

Another long pause.

"Good to know," I offered.

She got up. She took something out of her purse. In the parched post-sex darkness, it looked like a dead mouse. Then I realized it was the teabag from the restaurant; she had saved it in cellophane. The poor thing wanted to make herself some tea. As she moved around the darkened kitchen, I knew what she would know soon: I had no kettle.

In the darkness, I heard her give up. I closed my eyes, as if to sleep. And as she returned to the now-cold futon, I could hear her sigh. She released a heavy, knowing breath. For she knew that, in the morning, she would make me a nutritious breakfast that I would not eat. And she knew that she would leave her phone number written on the mirror in lipstick. And I would not call. I might think about it a few times. But I would not call.

And the next night, as she made herself dinner, she would

begin to cry. She would turn vulnerable. Someone's daughter. Their complicated pride and joy. She would have a little cry. She'd cry salty tears into her already salty miso soup. She would turn to her cat and say, "Well, Moribund, I did it again. I went home with an asshole."

# One Dumb Guy

We are one dumb guy, collectively. Individually, we are quite smart. But collectively, my comedy troupe, the Kids in the Hall, is like five guys on the street corner, blood sugar crashing, trying to decide where to eat. One's a vegetarian. One only eats meat. Two are dyslexic and one isn't eating, but still has a very strong opinion of where we should all go.

Shame stains, but pain fades with time. People's personal histories always seem so simple in the retelling. But in that retelling, the difficulty of each step is omitted. For us, every hurdle the Kids in the Hall faced, our bellies just barely cleared the bar. Scraping the top with a loud *thwang* as we pulled ourselves forward. Then, after that hurdle, we looked around, befuddled, wondering, "What's next?"

Scott accepted our offer to join the group. Or should I say, we never rejected his offer to join the group? Perhaps it felt to all of us, including Scott, that none of us had any say in the matter. It was just going to be the way it was supposed to be. With Scott, we became complete. We never put all our hands in a circle and said, "We're in this forever," like I think rock bands do. There were others who performed with us, but when the dust cleared, it was just the five of us who were standing together.

Scott was more than just a comic force of nature. In many ways, he was even more interesting to watch than Kevin. The way he would enter a meeting in mid-story—by which I mean, he was in the middle of a story, one that I guess he had told the first part of to some cab driver. He would wander to the food table eating three sandwiches while pulling out his wallet and placing it on the windowsill for some reason—it was hindering his storytelling, one would have to suppose. He would finish his story with a flourish.

Seven hours later, as we were walking home, he'd realize, "I can't find my wallet! Oh, and I've lost my passport too. I think I left it on the coffee table, at a party I went to last night."

Moreover, Scott was a ferocious performer who made us all try harder just to match him. There'd always been a sexual undertone to what we were doing, but Scott brought it to the surface.

We were five men obsessed with the world and our place in it. Comically, we worked well. But in other respects, we were "one dumb guy." We never did anything that made any sense businesswise. I'd like to think it was because we were punk, but the truth is, we were disorganized. Business wasn't a cool topic, and it was fun to disagree. Then as now, we were a band filled with bass players who thought they were all lead singers.

I remember troupes that had been together for only a few weeks opening shows for us. They'd have T-shirts to sell and mailing lists. We had nothing. One of us actually once said, during a business meeting, "We should get an agent to find opportunities for us that don't involve making money."

"What would he do?" I asked.

Long pause.

"Be our agent, of course."

"How would he, or we, make money?"

Another, even longer, pause.

Eventually, we did end up finding an agent. As I recall, we hired her because she wore a really funny pillbox hat. And when she took us out for lunch, she said to the waiter, "No, I don't want anything, thanks." Then stopped him. "Hold on, I changed my mind, I'll have a whole duck." She wasn't trying to be funny, but this was the funniest thing any of us had ever heard in our lives. To this day, we will say, "You know what? I'll have a whole duck." The point being, we used the "whole duck" as a reason to hire her. Not great business acumen. Even a man who once got 20 per cent in business college knows that.

We were doing semi-monthly shows at a Toronto club called the Rivoli, and they weren't going well. So I'd been sent in to convince the owners to let us do a show every week. The owners stared at me.

"You can't fill the place every other week, so your plan is . . . to do a show every week?"

"Yes!" I said enthusiastically, not realizing what a fool I was. Finally, they let us do it, after I promised we'd try harder and be funnier. Oh, and we would start "marketing." Marketing was a fancy word I knew from the hoity-toity community college I'd slunk out of.

We didn't try harder. Nor were we funnier. But we *did* market. We handed out fistfuls of two-for-one passes. We kept plugging away, and just when it seemed like we were out of gas, we caught on.

One night, the place was full. Yes! We had garnered a teeny-tiny following. After a few weeks of this, we decided to do a "real theatre run."

Mark became obsessed with the idea that, in this theatre show, we could score big by getting involved in the lucrative world of concessions. We could make a dollar a cookie.

"That's nothing to sneeze at."

But we lost money on the cookies. Scott ate most of them. Some, I think, he even sneezed on.

We were never dumber than when we were being scouted by *Saturday Night Live*. This theatre show had gotten a good review. So the next day, all of us were in the box office, pretending not to care about the review, and calculating how much money we were going to lose on the cookies, when the phone rang. I answered it. It was a producer from *Saturday Night Live* looking to get in touch with someone connected with the Kids in the Hall. Well, here I was.

She had great news. They were in town, scouting, and they were coming to our show! There would be four of them. Or maybe eight. Possibly ten. Of course, they needed tickets.

I explained the show was sold out. "Maybe next time? Although I'm not sure there will be a next time."

"Are you hearing me? This is *Saturday Night Live*. Don't you want us to see your show?"

"Sure, I do. But if you really wanted to see it so badly, you would have bought tickets like the other people did. We still have cookies for sale, though."

Silence. In my little punk mind, I thought that our show was for "the people." The people from *Saturday Night Live* were definitely not "the people."

This was my version of leaving my passport on the windowsill and then having to run back for it. After I hung up, I turned to the guys who had been huddled around the phone, listening. I explained what I'd just done. "Cool, right?"

I could see myself reflected in their faces. What an idiot I was. So I had to go figure out how to find the *Saturday Night Live* people and invite them to the show.

They came, and thus began an exciting and painful process for the troupe. In the end, they took Mark and me as writers. We would move to New York, and the rest of the guys would stay behind.

Only later did I realize that this would almost tear the troupe apart, although, ultimately, it brought us closer together.

I remember walking in to tell Mark we had gotten the *Saturday Night Live* job. He was working at Second Cup at the time. The first thing he said was, "I can't wait to tell my dad." This baffled me. It hadn't even crossed my mind to tell my father, and, in fact, I don't know if I ever told him.

On my first day at *SNL*, I heard, "Bruce, have you met Madonna?" I turned around, and it's Lorne Michaels, standing with the Material Girl herself.

"No, I don't think so." Feigning nonchalance, "Madonna, have we met?"

Later that day, I also got introduced to Timothy Leary, the grandfather of LSD. I complimented him on his "product" and told him it had helped me get through my tough teenage years. At that, he smiled. I thought, "*Saturday Night Live* is going to be the best place ever!" Sadly, it was mostly downhill from there.

I thought there'd be all these great minds melding together. But it didn't end up feeling that way. It was like being at a party where all the guests are really interesting, but somehow the party is not so "off the hook." These people, they weren't like Mark and me. And they were slowly realizing that we weren't like *them*.

I wrote a promo for the show: "Thirty Helens Agree." You know, archetypal fifty-year-old women, all named Helen? It would be thirty Helens in a field, saying, "*SNL* is better than we expected." The writers went crazy on me. First of all, how were they gonna get thirty Helens in a field? Second, it had to be fast and funny. Not slow and weird.

"'Better than expected'?! They should say it's hilarious. And, people don't know who these Helens are. They would have to be famous."

"Yes, but there's thirty of them. That oughta count for something."

They just stared.

In all seriousness, I asked, "Is it funnier if there are forty of them?"


One day, I was writing a sketch. I called one of the characters "Mr. Fake Name," which didn't sit well with an older writer. I actually argued with him that, "Mr. Fake Name doesn't sound fake to me." Watching him turn red, I realized that I was standing on a shrinking piece of ice. I muttered, "You don't get it"— first under, then over, my breath.

I rushed to the bathroom and put my head under the tap.

It was bad.

Mark came in and just watched me. I locked eyes with him, both of us knowing that I was going "under the rug" again.

Mark and I were secretly miserable. I snarfed coffee cake and drank Sam Adams beer every night. I put on my "freshman fifteen" and started wearing light-grey sweatpants I had bought on the street. (My freshman fifteen has since been whittled down to an elderly eleven, thanks to a lot of hard work and several fad diets like "raw foods" and "eating underwater.")

Mark and I lived together at the Chelsea Hotel. Which sounds cooler than it was. I remember Mark putting out little cardboard notes in our room that read, "Maids, please don't steal." It worked—they stopped stealing. Or at least, not stealing so much that we would notice.

We would fly the rest of the troupe into New York to come hang out and watch us work. Watching someone work is, ironically, laborious. But Mark and I thought it was a wonderful treat. We didn't realize it was painful for them. It was like flying your wife in to watch you make out with your mistress. Maybe worse, like making your mistress watch you getting it on with your wife. And of course, the troupe, in this case, was the wife.

Later, a plan was concocted. We were going to prove to everybody on the show how amazing we all were. Because, clearly, they weren't getting it. The Kids in the Hall were going to do a live stage show in New York!

And then the dreaded word was uttered: "showcase."

A showcase is traditionally where you perform for a lot of people you have begged to come see you. Then you invite a lot of people who really don't want to come see you, and you try to impress them. I'm exaggerating—there's also a smattering of tipsy tourists. As there was on this night.

As the place half-filled up, I thought, "Finally! Finally, they are going to see us unleash our 'us-ness.' Finally, they'll understand."

The show didn't go great, but we still had our big ender in our back pocket. At the time, we'd been dining out on an epic piece called 'The Suburbs' in which, you guessed it, we ripped the lid off of the suburbs. In it, Kevin and I stood apocalyptically under a sheer curtain and implored the audience to "look into our eyes (even though they couldn't actually see our eyes because of the curtain) and sense the power of the suburbs."

Kevin and I stood in the kitchen, waiting for our cue. Okay, it was a theatre that served food. A bar, I guess you could call it. We looked at each other. This was it! We put the curtain that had been brought in from Canada over our heads. We walked out. Trying not to trip, we made our way to the area on the floor that was meant to be the stage.

"I want you to look into my eyes and sense the power of the suburbs."

Disinterest, mixed with coughing. A shaky start, but we'd get there.

One of the vignettes in this epic is of a dad. He sits in his suburban easy chair. Eating off his TV tray. (Take *that*, New York!) He has just learned his son is gay, and he has a nightmare. He imagines his son having sex with a cruel, leather-clad German. But on this night, we had decided to take this vignette one step further. We did not want to merely tap dance on the edge, we wanted to do push-ups on it. So, breaking the number one rule of showcases—"Don't do untried material"—we added a new character. A character called the AIDS Fairy. He came out and sprinkled the son and his lover with "AIDS dust" (water-soaked paper) pulled from an "AIDS bucket" (a trash can with "AIDS bucket" written on the side, stolen from the Chelsea Hotel—now we were even).

As additional interactive theatre, the AIDS Fairy also threw this wet, unwanted AIDS dust at the audience. The late-eighties audience, filled with people whose loved ones were dying of AIDS, and industry people. Oh, and a few tipsy tourists. Could you imagine a worse group?

In the silence, I heard one of the actors from *SNL*, who'd been roped into coming, say to his girlfriend, "McCulloch will never make a buck in the business."

After the TV season was over, we went home.

In the end, the troupe forgave our "dalliance." After a short frosty period, they embraced us again. Then Lorne came to Toronto and saw us all perform. He said, "Maybe you guys should do your own TV show. Ever thought of that?" And even to one dumb guy, that seemed like a really good idea.

# *Vigil*

When I think about suicide—not that I think about suicide—I don't think about how I'd do it, but how I would write the note. You see, my handwriting is so terrible that people wouldn't be able to understand my dark decision.

"Why did he do it?"

"Let me try and read his note . . . Maybe something about 'goody buys crappy warpaint'?" (Goodbye cruel world.)

But if I didn't write a note by hand, what would I do? Put it on my computer? That seems sort of cold. Well, suicide is a cold and selfish act, but still. A suicide note on a computer is like someone emailing you flowers. Not so touching. (Unless you've emailed me flowers, then thanks, yours were different.) If I did put it on my computer, what would I call the file? "Note"? Or "Suicide"? I wouldn't want my writing assistant to stumble across it one day as she was cleaning up my desktop.

"Bruce, what is this?"

"Oh, just a new idea I'm tinkering with."

Would I then, to keep up with the times, make a heartfelt suicide video? Or how about a nice, up-tempo "My life is shit, I'm in a pit" kind of music video? Okay, just 'cause I'm thinking about it now, doesn't mean I'm thinking about it. Or would I do this all on film? I mean, it's more expensive, but it just looks better. Makes your eyes look warmer. Kind of old-school cool, right? What would a budget for a suicide note video be? It wouldn't kill me to crunch some numbers. Could I apply for a grant for such a thing? And if I did, how long would I have to wait to hear back from the suicide grant people? And maybe if I could get a grant to make a suicide music video, I wouldn't even feel like killing myself in the first place. Not that I ever feel like killing myself.

I was thinking about all of this on the plane ride to Seattle. The *Kids in the Hall* show had been on the air about a year and we were on tour. We were performing in Seattle the next night. Kurt Cobain had just offed himself, so suicide was on our mind. Scott knew for sure that Kurt had planned to come to see our show. He had no actual knowledge of this, but he just "knew." As assuredly as Scott knew that Kurt was a "big, big" fan of ours. Truthfully, I don't think Kurt was even a "small, small" fan of ours, but I didn't want to burst Scott's dark bubble. Scott said if, the next night at the show, he looked out into the audience and there was an empty seat, we would know "that was Kurt's."

The next night at the show, as we looked out, there were plenty of Kurts. Most of the balcony and scattered throughout the floor were several Kurts. I blame the promoter for not spending more on advertising.

We heard people talking about the vigil the moment we got off the plane. Honestly, I didn't really know what a vigil was. I had some idea, though, that it involved candles. The lighting of candles, the making and breaking of eye contact, sad shrugs and words that weren't like "hmmm" or "ahhh."

I'd never been to a vigil. At that point in my life, I had never even been to a funeral. Well, I'd been to some bad parties that people said reminded them of funerals. But there was no corpse, unless you counted the food table, where people would pause, shake their heads and move on. The closest thing to a funeral? Three turtles I flushed down the toilet in 1972. After they died in 1971.

A vigil isn't even a funeral. It's like going to a drive-in with no screen.

The bluest skies I've ever seen weren't in Seattle. The greenest hills I've ever seen weren't in Seattle. When my silly-skit troupe arrived in that coastal town, there were only shades of grey. Anyway, we arrived in Seattle ninety minutes prior to Kurt's vigil. I hate to admit it, but for a selfish, confused instant, I thought the attention might have been about us. But no, they did not want to "crush our heads." Or even have us sign our own faces on pictures they held.

I saw two young guys holding a placard with a picture of Kurt on it. I studied it. Locking eyes with a cardboard Cobain. He looked little, long-haired, alone and powerful, like Mother Theresa must have looked in her twenties. His eyes said to me that he wanted to be somewhere else.

And I guess he had gone there.

Our Seattle van driver told me about a good place to eat steak and that he'd driven Kurt on New Year's Eve and that he was "really messed up." But they always say that. Whomever they drive anywhere, ever, is always "really messed up." Which really meant that he was probably quiet or didn't tip so well.

I could just see two girls in a Seattle suburb—if Seattle even had suburbs; I didn't know, I had just landed. I hadn't even eaten my steak yet. I could just see two teenage girls in a Seattle suburb: "What are ya gonna wear to the vigil?"

"Well, black, of course."

"But, what would *he* want me to wear?"

"Plaid. Dirty hair. Arlene. For real: do *not* wash your hair."

In my hotel room, I just stared into the distance. Well, all right, I'm lying: I watched TV. I was torn between a nap and going down to the square. I just didn't know if I was in the mood to see beautiful seventeen-year-old children in dreadlocks, white hippies celebrating his dark demise. Cynicism is my whiskey, so I had a few:

"Are the other two guys gonna get a new singer? Robert Plant could use a job."

"Do they split the money differently, now that they are down to two?"

"I guess that Courtney Love album just sold about two million copies."

"Would the square be full if he had simply slipped on a small hotel soap, gargled his tongue and was gone?"

Truthfully, what if he hadn't been a beautiful, blue-eyed, black-hearted blond boy? What if he'd looked like Aaron

Neville? I think there would be sixty people, max. And perhaps they would move the vigil to a smaller location—even the Sea Vista Ballroom in my hotel. If the vigil had been in my hotel, I might have popped by. Stuck my head in. But it wasn't, so I decided not to go.

Instead, I fell asleep watching *Jeopardy!* The life-affirming *ding* when contestants pressed their buttons, eager to answer. They wanted to be part of the world. Why didn't he?

Don't get me wrong. Someone forlorn and confused had done something stupid and left a lot of stronger people behind. There was not a lot else to be said.

The next day, I went for a run along the ocean. Well, I went for a run on an asphalt path along the ocean. Twenty minutes in, something up a hill caught my eye. As I sprinted towards it, I could soon make out what it was. Someone had taken some wood—long cedar planks—and with them spelled out the words "Bye Kurt."

I took a big Seattle breath, looked up at the city and wondered, "What didn't he see?" I thought of a little boy grown up. Now gone.

And I whispered, "Bye Kurt."

And if I've ever been to a vigil, I guess that was it.

# Sharing Air

We are connected

By our breath.

We are sharing air.

Through air, we are connected

To all those we will never know.

So in a way, I am a teenage goth girl with daddy issues.

I am an old man who misses the war.

I am a bass player who just can't find the right band

And I am a band that can't find a bass player.

I am a Boston Pizza waitress who strips

For her cat.

I am the dude going into "cash for car titles,"

Hoping that Ski-Doos count.

I am Elvis making love to an Elvis impersonator,

Wondering, "Which one am I?"


I am a beautiful girl with ugly feet,

Knowing it's much better than the opposite.

I am the stressed-out dad in a minivan wishing

There was someone darker than the Devil

That I could pray to.

I am the empty elevator.

When the elevator stops,

The doors open and no one gets in.

That is me.


I am roadkill at the side of the road

Whose last words were "I think I can make it Mur—"

(I think he was saying Murray).

I am the guy who loves the girl but will never have her.

The closest I will ever come to sleeping with her

Is the feel of her mattress on my face

As I help her move . . .

We are connected. By our breath.

Air never ages

And is never destroyed.

So you have breathed the same air as Kafka,

The beatniks,

The Rat Pack,

The Beastie Boys.

Everyone you have loved and lost.

Or "blown it" with.

All the people,

All the pets,

They are still there,

In the air.

If you miss them,

Just take a breath . . .

# Good Investment

They say that if you want to get to know someone, go out with them. I disagree. I say if you want to get to know someone, break up with them. Oh, you'll get to know them real quick.

That's a joke I used to tell when I did standup and had something called an "act." But it was based in truth. I remember realizing this when I was lying in the house I had just moved into. Alone.

I'd been living with a woman in her house. She was older.

I think it's time to admit that I have always had a thing for older women. There's a cliché—"If you want to know what the girl you are thinking of marrying is going to end up looking like, take a peek at her mother." And I would always think, "Why wait? Just date the mother."

So I'd been living with a slightly older woman, yet for some reason I'd gone out and bought a house just like the one we were living in. Curious, right? I told her what I had told myself: that it was a "good investment." At hearing this, her kind face quivered. She realized then what I would know soon—that I was leaving her.

So we broke up. Slowly at first, then all of a sudden.

Which is how all breakups always go.

I didn't just leave her, I left my crucifixion machine. How many of us can say that? It was from our silly-skit show. A scene called "Dr. Seuss Bible," where a Seussian Jesus gets crucified on a cartoonish Rube Goldberg–style machine.

"Forgive them," Jesus says. "They know not what they do, for they wander this world in toe-crampity shoes."

The machine was huge. It was bright. Not at all the clean, elegant design the woman had favoured. Or even "shabby chic," which was all the rage at the time. I'd had to hire three men to carry it in and not tell them what it was, being a crucifixion machine and all.

But the woman didn't stop me. The machine stayed. And

remained. It blocked all the light that poured into her otherwise tasteful Victorian home.

But after I left, I'm sure she stared up at that yellow cross, a cruel reminder of what I had done to her. I'm so comically dark that, even now, I find it kind of funny.

But you are a reader of stories; you know how things twist. I would end up getting mine . . .

I found myself alone in my "good investment." Not feeling invested in it at all. When I first bought the house, I didn't move into it for months. So when I finally arrived, all the neighbours gathered 'round to see who was coming to join their neighbourhood. How disappointed they must have been when it was just me getting out of a cab. A coffeemaker under my arm. Oh, right, I also had my little cowboy boots tucked under the other arm.

Me, my coffeemaker and I.

I spent days lying on my sheetless bed, wondering what I had done. The worst part about the house was its location—it was right near my bed. I'd wake up in the morning and I'd be in the house. Also terrible, the house was in a nice family neighbourhood. I was not a family. I was the pie-faced weirdo from the silly-skit show who came and went at gruesome hours. Blaring Hüsker Dü all the goddamned time.

I never pulled my weeds. I actually mistook them for perfectly good trees. Someone pulled them out and left them in a hostile pile while I lay sleeping one afternoon. In front of my place, I had a rented car that I never drove. It had parking tickets piled up on the windshield. I was told via anonymous letter it was an "eyesore."

Honestly, I tried to fit in. I smiled at my neighbours. I smiled at their children. I'd watch their "everyone plays, everyone wins, non-competitive" baseball games. I'd even shout the occasional "'Atta boy!" I learned that, in this modern era, you're not allowed to cheer for a specific kid, or even a team, but rather the sport itself.

"Go, baseball!"

In truth, I didn't fit in because I wasn't part of a family. I wasn't like everyone else in the neighbourhood. Doing things as "a family." Pushing people aside on the sidewalk and saying, "Get out of my way, I have to get a perfect turkey for my family!"

"We need family time!"

"Family is the most important thing!"

No, it's not. I came from one.

What is a family? A tyrannical klatch of people who look like you but are nothing like you. A family is something you survive.

All those cruel little self-obsessed units. All the zombies with their arms outstretched, taking pictures that they already have.

Does a family have to be the people you were born into? I think a family can be whatever we want to create. Why can't a family be every record Johnny Cash ever recorded? What's wrong with being part of a close-knit phone-sex community? Or a widower and his new boyfriend who cooks for you every Sunday? A Pilates instructor who lets you come over drunk, "no questions asked"? One of those questions being, "Who is the *other* Pilates instructor you sometimes visit?" Why not a rose garden, a parrot and a vibrator? Or perhaps, a little man and a poodle?

Speaking of transitions . . . I had bought a poodle the previous month in a bout of ennui. Okay, I'm lying. I was hungover.

I called a breeder, a keeper of dogs from broken homes, and I said, "I'm lonely. What've you got?" There was only a poodle. I didn't want a poodle, but I thought I should meet her anyway, thinking she might be a gateway to better dogs. I had told myself that whatever I did, I would not come home with this dog.

Cut to: me in a cab with a poodle.

I was now living alone with a poodle I wasn't so sure about, who wasn't so sure about me. When we got home, I phoned the breeder and said, "I don't know if this is going to work out. We're not getting along."

The breeder asked, "Are you talking to her?"

"No."

"You have to talk to her all the time, you know."

I muttered that of course I knew that, even though I didn't. I hung up and turned to the dog. "So . . . how was your day?"

She just stared at me.

I'd ask, "Are you hungry?" Then I'd feed her and she would eat.

"Let's go for a walk." And she'd agree.

We'd go out, and I'd tell her about my feelings and what silly skit I was working on. We were like a rom-com where it was frosty at first, but by the one-hour mark, we had really fallen for each other.

Then I learned that she had been lying about her age. As women sometimes do. When I got her, the breeder told me she was three. But when she developed a limp, I took her to the vet. He took an X-ray and announced she was seven. I stared at my dog. This was a partial death sentence. All the years we wouldn't have together. This dog was also turning out to be not such a good investment.

Oddly, though, this deception brought us closer together. We were now living on borrowed time. Like a Romeo and Juliet who have already seen the play they are starring in. We became inseparable. My friends starting calling her "Wife."

She and I would jaunt out into the family neighbourhood, day after day, finally feeling more a part of things. We would wave at the children we encountered. And now, they would wave back. One day on our walk, I noticed a flyer on a telephone pole. It was for a play that very weekend at the local grade school. *Joseph and the Amazing Technicolor Dreamcoat*. "Well, I'm a lonely man," I thought. "I have nothing to do on Saturday. And I love silly things. This is the trifecta." Seeing a school production of *Joseph and the Amazing Technicolor Dreamcoat* seemed like the best thing I could possibly do with of my weekend.

So I had my assistant phone and get me a ticket, "Yes, just one. I know; we think it's sad too. Don't tell anyone, but he had this great woman and he just left her. No reason . . ."

I must admit, I was really looking forward to the play. It was four days away. I could barely wait. I lay in bed in anticipation, "Wife" beside me. Things were looking up. I now had sheets on my bed. They were the wrong size, but my assistant wasn't good at everything. She did get me that ticket, though.

The night of the play, I took my seat, early and eagerly. I have to say, even though my expectations were extremely high, the show delivered. And then some! I sat there, wishing I was a theatre reviewer so I could give it a rave. The only confusing part was that they had rotating Josephs. But why wouldn't they? I'm sure everyone in that talent-laden grade school would want to play that meaty role. The third Joseph was my favourite. She was actually a young Asian girl. Quick on her feet and brimming with soul.

As the lights went up for intermission, I stayed in my seat, still scribbling notes in my program for the imaginary review I was now writing. A few people came over. Of course, I presumed they wanted an autograph. "My pen! My pen!" I thought. But nope, they didn't want my autograph. They wondered why I was there. The principal had arrived and explained that the production was for "friends and family only."

"Well, you got me there. I'm not either of those."

"Then why are you here?" the principal asked.

"Well, I'm here . . . because I like children."

Long pause.

In retrospect, I wish I'd thought a little longer before I said that. Because I realized what should have had been obvious:

for the last few minutes, they were accusing me of liking children. *Really* liking children.

Then some cruel bastard—I assume he was a math teacher—said, "Obviously, you're a pedophile. I've seen you with your poodle, prancing around, smiling at kids!" As I left, I turned back and said to him, "Sir, you are wrong. That is no poodle, that is my wife. Not all families are the same."

# Nursey Says

I'd gone to see the doctor, but I went back to see his nurse. There was something about the way she'd taken my blood pressure that made my blood pressure go up.

I was in Vancouver. My skit troupe would be performing there in a couple of days. But till then, we had all scattered, happy to have a break from each other after a long tour. So I convinced Nursey to go out for a bite.

We were in a restaurant. It was 10 p.m. on a Sunday. I thought the evening was just winding down, but apparently not. Nursey opened her purse and took something out.

"Take this."

"No, thanks," I replied.

"I know what I'm doing. I'm a nurse."

She *was* a nurse. Even though it was clearly her night off. I looked at the little pill in her beautiful hand.

I protested. "Isn't dope for dopes? That's what the commercials say."

She just rolled her big brown eyes.

"Trust me."

And as you may remember, I never trust a person who says, "Trust me." And this is the night I learned that.

I took the pill.

That night, I did what Nursey told me to do until I couldn't do it any longer. I wanted to please her. She was special in that way that you think no guy but you can see. Although, in truth, every guy in the world sees it.

She had "the night flowing through her." I say this corny thing because it was one of the things she said, later on. Although, when *she* said it, it didn't sound so bad.

"Some drugs you use to get away from yourself. This is not one of those drugs." She leaned in. "Okay, I'll let you in on a secret. It's about love."

Then she took her fingernail and wrote the word "love" on

my forearm. I think it's still there. "Let's pay up," she said, grabbing her see-through purse that didn't appear to have any money in it. When a beautiful woman says, "Let's pay up," it means "You pay up." I paid up, tipped well—as I think Nursey would have wanted me to—and followed her out.

She thrust her hand in the air. Immediately, a cab stopped. Like they do in movies. She waited for me to open the door for her, then turned to me quite seriously.

"Soon there will be a lot of information coming at you."

"Will it hurt?" I joked, hoping to lighten the mood.

"Only if you don't know yourself. It's like you'll create a map of yourself. Inside of you."

Ugh, if she could have seen inside of me at that moment. Inside, there was cynicism. Rivers and roads where cynicism flowed and frolicked. Cynicism had always protected me. Especially from saying stupid things like "love" out loud.

Of course, I loved people. Us with our silly little dreams, plans and projects that seldom work out. As a closet Oprah enthusiast, I have often cried watching an episode about, for example, a single mom who found her "true" calling, prompting Oprah to give her a van. Or, say, if I see twins who have a lemonade stand and it's a rainy day, so no one's buying any. Seeing their disappointed faces crushes me. I want to run up and give them a hundred dollars. But I have grown cautious since the *Amazing Technocolor Dreamcoat* debacle.

A girlfriend once told me that I loved people, but not necessarily one at a time. I forget her name right now—proving perhaps, she was right. See, some people think, "A stranger is a friend you haven't met yet." I've always thought that a friend is an enemy who hasn't betrayed you yet.

Nursey and I went to see a band. They were okay. I was so relieved that the drug wasn't working.

"But how do I tell her it's not working?" I thought to myself.

"Tell me *what's* not working?" asked Nursey.

Oh. I guess I said that out loud instead of merely thinking it. Perhaps the drug *was* working.

Suddenly the "okay" band became really good. Their music was liquid, if you know what I mean. Uh-oh. Why is someone tapping me on the back of the neck with fingers both warm and cold. How did someone slip peppermint into my spine without me seeing?

"I think it's working," I said to her.

She just stared at me. Oh, I guess I didn't say that one out loud. I only thought it. Or maybe I did say it? We just stared at each other. After our silent conversation ended, she grabbed me by the hand.

"I have two things to tell you. One, drink a lot of water or your organs will shut down. And two, we're leaving now."

Then she asked why I looked so pensive. I told her I was trying to think of everyone I knew, in alphabetical order. She smiled, said, "Good," and we left to go and look for a rave. Yes, I was going to a rave. Nursey's powers were infinite.

As we approached the door, I was scared they'd ask me for ID. I knew full well I was too old to go to a rave. But they let me in anyway.

The music . . . honestly, not my favourite. Nothing rhymes. No words you can hum at work. But that night, I liked it. Its irritable scramble was oddly comforting.

Nursey screamed in my ear so I could hear her over the hateful lovable music. "Don't worry. I'm going to take care of you, but I have to leave you. I need to go share a brain with the DJ."

She smiled as if I knew what that meant.

I found myself sitting outside a chill-out room, caressing the corduroy pants of a guy I hadn't yet met. I introduced myself, explaining that I was reading his pants. He was flattered. I learned that he was a tree planter on a tree-free day. Other tree planters and club kids were now staring at me. They recognized me from my silly-skit show. They wanted my autograph. I wanted theirs.

"Why are you here?" they asked.

"To meet you, of course."

They liked that answer. Little did I realize they would soon be turning on me.

"We never thought we'd meet you in a place like this, but we always felt you were one of us."

"I am," I said. Not knowing what I was stepping into.

I felt several sets of eyes on me.

"We are on the red path," the noblest one, with the soft, floating face, said.

"I'm on the red path too," I lied, presuming the red path had something to do with Mao or fat-tire biking in Moab.

They cooed with excitement. The corduroy I was caressing melted.

"It is so great that you're here and you're not on drugs."

"Excuse me?" I said or thought.

We smiled for a good long while.

Then I actually said for sure, "What makes you think I'm not on drugs?"

"Because you're on the red path. Clear body, mind and spirit. We used to come to raves on drugs all the time. When we were just kids. But now we're on the red path. Like you."

I just said the first thing that came to mind. "I have always thought that the love I feel has trouble leaving my body. Do you ever think that?"

They warmly agreed.

"I also thought that if someone didn't get one of my jokes, it was okay because it would travel over their heads and fly to the end of the universe, and wait for me there. I find great comfort in that."

They laughed.

Then I said, "I am not a *Star Trek* fan."

Long pause.

"But remember that *Star Trek* episode where Spock operates on his own brain? That's how I feel right now."

Their smiles started to falter. Then, trying to correct things, I added, "Well, there is one thing I know for sure: the aliens did *not* want corners put in people's bedrooms. They know how lonely staring up at corners can make us."

My new friends whispered and mumbled. "He's on drugs."

They turned into teen cops and made me confess.

"Okay, I did it. I took drugs. Just this once."

The rave children were so upset.

"Nursey told me it was the right thing to do. Blame Nursey!"

They had just met me and I had already betrayed them. This was a record, even for me.

"I don't trust myself," I said. "I am going to have myself followed. Just in case."

This was no help. As my new friend got up to go, I implored him to "take his pants but leave the corduroy behind," knowing that I would need it later.

He did not.

As they took their beautiful and wise eyes away from me, I promised that one day I'd plant trees with them. None of us believed me anymore.

I float-stormed off to find Nursey. I found her in a ball-filled kiddie pool. She didn't look much like a nurse at all. I was trying not to freak out. She looked at me and said, "Don't freak out."

"I have to," I explained. "These kids are freaking me out. They believed in me before they met me, but not after they met me."

She scolded, "Don't tell me that! Your freaking out is freaking me out!"

A tear rolled down her cheek and she spat out, "This drug

isn't all it's cracked up to be. It's like trying to stand up on a fucking wave sometimes."

"What?! What about love and maps of our insides?"

She pulled me in beside her.

I was now in a ball-filled kiddie pool with a disgraced nurse at 4 a.m.

She said, "Okay, there's a part I didn't tell you about, before the part I *did* tell you about. You're starting to understand yourself. Which in your case, may not be a good thing." Then she said, "I'm leaving."

She just lay there, staring at me. After a moment, I realized this meant I was supposed to leave. As I did, she said, "Whatever you do, don't look in the mirror."

Jump cut to: me in my hotel room, cross-legged on the bathroom counter, looking in the mirror. The mirror looking back at me. Hard. A slew of questions screaming through my head:

"Who cheers up the cheerleaders?"

"Do I have insomnia because I can't forgive myself?"

"What would I need forgiveness for?"

Then, "Sleep is remembrance. Breath is forgiveness."

It was now 9 a.m. in Toronto, so I phoned my agent's office. Into the answering machine, I said, "I need to tell you about this new idea, sleep is remembrance. Breath is forgiveness." My agent, arriving for work, picked up the phone.

"Bruce, is this some sort of joke?"

"No, I had a run-in with some tree planters. I've let them down. Soon the entire forest will know."

"Do you need me to call a doctor?"

"No, I've already consulted a nurse."

Long pause. Then I leaned into the phone, comforted by the amplified sound of my own breath. My agent breathed back. I could feel her breath slow down. It calmed me. Our breathing was now in tandem.

Then I said, "Did you know that sometimes the love I feel has trouble leaving my body?"

She said, "Yes. Everyone knows that about you . . ."

# Jean Jacket Love

My first older woman. She was only eleven months my senior, but when you are in grade eight, that is a decade. Her hair shone from the expensive shampoo that her "good family" could afford. Not the jumbo bottle of Woolco bargain brand that was in our bathroom. Susan M. was tall and blonde with beautiful hair that you never saw her brush. She was car-stoppingly pretty, but even more importantly, she was kind. I could feel her caring heart thump away beneath her gingham crop top. Also, luckily for me, she was my first love.

If the first person you love is kind, it's almost as powerful as having a good family. Because your family trains you for the world. But your "first" trains you for love.

Susan and I were in love. Jean jacket love. We'd hold hands as we walked the streets of Calgary. We'd stop and hold on to the cuffs of each other's jean jackets, staring into the other's eyes. Me looking up slightly; the kink in my neck barely registering. Sometimes we would stop staring and kiss. Sometimes we would stop kissing and talk. But then, we'd talk about how we should go back to necking.

When we left each other at the end of each day, we'd exchange jean jackets because we still wanted to be together. Wrapped in each other. C'mon, we were teenagers.

Her jean jacket had a rainbow crocheted across the back, but I didn't care. It was hers. I waited for someone to mention the silly girly rainbow, so I could defend our love. In her honour, I could bust some heads. But no one ever mentioned it. Maybe because of the way I smiled when I wore that jacket. The way I never smile today. I try to smile in pictures. Honestly, I do. In pictures I now use what friends call "my Facebook face." Not then. I smiled whenever I thought about my sweet first love, Susan M., which was all the time.

I craved everything about her. Her handwriting—I could have made love to her handwriting. It was so fluid and pretty, soft and curvy. Like her.

She drank tea. So I drank tea. She stirred it with her always perfectly tanned hands. We'd go to her house after school. I think I loved that house as much as I loved Susan. So calm you could hear the cuckoo clock they owned. No yelling. Just quiet. This wasn't what I was used to. I came from a rye-fuelled, slap-and-blame, shoddy wreck of a townhouse. A dog chained up, ready to bite you if you walked in. Or out.

But in her house, Susan M. and I listened to the quiet, drank tea and memorized each other's faces.

In her house was the soft purr of a humidifier. I remember staring at the mist that billowed past us as we grabbed each other's jean jackets and necked once her mother left the room. And sometimes *before* her mother left the room. Mrs. M. was an older, and just as nice, version of Susan M. Her dad was a nice guy too. And what was even better, he was always off at work.

Day after day, we'd fall asleep on the couch, safely nestled in each other's arms. But then I'd bolt awake, thinking, "Wake up quick—she's right beside you!" My life was . . . perfect.

You were in young love once. You know where this is headed. Trouble.

One morning, Susan M. ran outside, where I sat waiting on a bench that had been placed there for me to sit and wait on.

She could barely breathe. I kissed her for a minute or two, to calm her down and because I hadn't seen her in a few hours. Finally, she told me her family had great news. But it was terrible news for us. They were moving. Her dad had got a job in Willowdale, which I soon realized was in the greedy province of Ontario. A place, in my mind, as cold and as nasty as it actually is.

The countdown began. Sixty days quickly melted into five nights as we held each other up on "The Hill." The Hill, where other teenagers necked and now we just held each other in our slow-moving car crash of a love story. No music could describe what we were feeling. No parents understood what we were going through.

Soon it would be Willowdale Day. Our only comfort was that we'd one day be together again. When I turned eighteen, I'd get a job at a gas station to support us. If I wasn't already a rock star. By then, she would be in veterinary school. She'd bring home puppies to lick our faces just as we'd lick each other's. And yes, we'd have a baby.

We exchanged jean jackets one final time.

After she left town, I stormed into my parents' living room, where they were eating dinner and watching TV. I screamed at them, "You are both so stupid! You don't know anything! You are cattle. Cattle no one would even eat!"

I went into the bathroom and locked the door. For some reason, I threw all our putrid pink shampoo down the bathtub drain. I took my dad's Mark Ten cigarettes and lit a fire in the toilet.

Then I waited . . .

A few days later, the first of a hundred inch-thick, jasmine-scented letters arrived. I hated the postmark that read "Willowdale," but I devoured every one. In my room, door locked, her words would flow over me. What she was doing. What she was thinking. She described every object in her room. Her life. Her new Bruce-less life. I was with her, except I was not. I would write her back, describing my empty days without her. My letters were much shorter. My handwriting choppy but brave. Brave but wavering. The smell on her jean jacket grew faint. And one day, her letters stopped.

Over time, Susan M. turned from my first great love into merely "a story." She was now just a name.


People in our own mythology become just names at a certain point, and you kind of forget them. What they meant to you.

We always remember how we got the scars, but seldom the skin before the scars.

Many years later, when my silly-skit show started, Susan M. got hold of me. It barely registered. "Oh, I get it, now that I'm on TV, people are crawling out of the woodwork." I asked my Little Friend, whom I had known since I was teenager—my Little Friend who was now a Little Man—if I should see her.

"Yes, you need to see her."

"Why?"

"Because after she left, you sort of became an asshole for a few years."

I took this as a "comp-u-sult" (half-compliment, half-insult). An insult because he was calling me an asshole, but a compliment because he was implying I wasn't one anymore.

Then I started to think back. After she left is when I started fighting. When I say "fighting," it suggests I did okay. But actually, I would get in fights and just get thumped. After she left, I starting gobbling acid (and if my kids are reading this, "acid" means a really big lollipop). Should I see her? At the time, I was adrift with myself, my family-less self. So why not?

She came over to my house. My "good investment." It was weird, because she had an old version of her young pretty face.

She was still beautiful, but I couldn't see the girl in her. Turns out, she was happily married and still living in Willowdale. The place I had hated so much. And obviously now, for good reason.

We had an awkward tea. She got serious for a moment. I thought, "Is she going to hit me up for money?" People on TV don't make as much as you think they do, you know? She talked about the jasmine-scented letters and why they had stopped.

"You don't know?" she asked. "He told me you knew."

It turns out that my dad, worn bare by my sadness and rants, had made the decision to call Susan M.'s house. Her parents answered and my dad informed them that Susan should not write anymore. He explained I had a new girlfriend and not to drag me down any longer. And finally, that I had asked him to call and "end things" for me. None of that was true, of course.

"Oh, that's what happened," I said half-heartedly, not feeling much. Then Susan told me she'd had dreams about me her entire life. In the dreams, she wasn't sure if I was okay. And she couldn't get to me. To help me and love me the way she had when we were kids. So she had to come see me. She needed to see if I was okay. Well, here I was, a sort of grown man. I was and wasn't okay.

I told her, "Of course I'm okay. C'mon, I'm doing great!"

Those eyes looked into me. The tea was over.

I walked her out to her car. Her white Jetta. I've since realized it's the car of women who are prizes but don't seem to know it. Truly, that should be in the ads.

As I was saying goodbye to her, I went to give her a careful little hug, and instinctively I grabbed for the cuffs of her jean jacket.

They were not there.

I took her hands instead. Then my hands went around her back. The back I knew and now remembered. We held each other. Then collapsed. The neighbours walked by as we hugged for twenty minutes and cried. And cried.

In the time since she left for Willowdale, I had never cried for her. I had only yelled. Only lit a few toilet fires, smashed the glass on a few cigarette machines and got the bad end of some fights.

The tears I had never cried had become a wave. With her again, they flowed and flowed. I felt like I was in love with her again. But I wasn't in love with her. What I was feeling was her love, leaving my body. And then my own love followed. Flooding out, finally.

Next time, little boy, cry that tear.

# *Radiohead*

"How do you feel about marriage and children?" I screamed into the ear of the Unimpressed Girl I was with.

"What? I can't hear you."

I guess she couldn't hear me over the haunting dirge that is Radiohead.

"I was just curious . . . How do you feel about marriage and children?"

She looked at me and laughed. It *did* seem like a non sequitur, it being our first date and all.

We were four hours into a five-hour date and it was going badly. And great. Great for me. Badly for her. A lurching night if ever there was one.

"Marriage and kids?" she stammered, "Seriously? I guess anything is possible for anyone. Depending on what the people who are having that conversation think of things."

Literally the vaguest answer of all time. I realized I was on the verge of appearing like, or actually being, a creep.

I couldn't help myself. That night, the Unimpressed Girl came over me like a golden shadow. A shadow that did not seem to notice me. For me, it wasn't love at first sight, but love at first night. But it was one-sided, as if I was ejaculating into a whirring fan.

She half-smiled and turned back to the band. I watched the back of her head for a while. Radiohead are pretty dull. Especially on a bad night—and I think this was one. We were in a huge airplane hangar. Me, some Radiohead fans and an Unimpressed Girl whom I was blowing it with. When the next song was over (I wasn't really sure if it was over—or if it was even a song, for that matter), I tried another tactic: "Do you want to get out of here?"

She looked at me quizzically. "No. Radiohead's my favourite band."

"Oh," I back-pedalled, "I don't want to get out of here, either! I was just making sure you wanted to stay. Radiohead is my favourite band too!"

"Cool. What's your favourite album?"

I couldn't think of the names of any Radiohead albums.

Long, long pause.

"This one," I finally said, in reference to the song that was playing, which made about as much sense as the other things I'd said that night.

She looked at me like I was an old fool, then turned back to the band . . .

She had passed the "jukebox test" I'd given her earlier, when we had started the night with a cautious beer. I'd escorted her to the jukebox, plugged in the quarters and asked, "What would you like to play? The Buzzcocks or Journey?"

It's a trick question. The correct answer being Journey. Any cool fool can play the Buzzcocks. And of course, on a desert island, the Buzzcocks would be the right answer. But this was not a desert island. This was a bar that served inedible food but had a good jukebox. Only someone so cool that they didn't care if they seemed cool or not could play Journey. She pressed the buttons and Journey blared. As she moved her shoulders to the music, Journey never sounded, or looked, so good. She had passed the test that others had failed.

She also passed my "dress test."

I've bought enough dresses with enough women to know that they should just know. They should come out of the change room, glance in the mirror and say, "Yes! This dress is perfect. I don't even need to look at the price tag." They shouldn't come out of the change room puckering their face, saying, "I like it, but is mustard really my colour?" Well, mustard isn't really *anyone's* colour. They shouldn't have to be convinced. Or convince themselves.

This, of course, is an analogy to love. A woman shouldn't say, "I like Derrick, he's a nice guy. He takes good care of himself. I feel safe when I'm with him." She should say, "I want me some Derrick. Me wait outside Derrick house. Me no need no sleep. Just Derrick." On sight, I had felt "yes" about her. But she did not feel the same about me. Oh well, live and fail.

The date had been a setup. A friend of mine who owed me three hundred dollars thought I'd forgive the debt if he set me up with a nice girl. We both knew my history, that I'd always blown it with the "nice ones." I'd actually broken the hearts of two girls named Karen the previous year. What are the odds? Actually, pretty good. I'd be—or seem—interested in a certain woman and just fade away. I'd get in my own head, think about what I wanted to do next, and the next thing I knew, it was two months later and I had blown it.

But I was getting older now. I had made a change that was invisible, even to me. There was caution now to what once had come naturally.

As a young man, I never thought too much about relationships. I just followed the frayed map that I'd been handed in childhood. My map had bumpy dirt roads, where other people's maps had highways with bright green road signs that said "Marriage and Children."

When I was young, I had no interest in being part of a couple. All those hopeless, paired-up fools. As the world goes marching two by two. People pairing up. Finishing each other's sentences. Sharing one brain. "Honey, what did *we* think of that film?" Couples where she cuts his hair and it looks like shit, but it doesn't matter, because they're not going anywhere. Couples getting fat, but it doesn't matter, because they're getting exactly as fat as each other. Shopping. Discussing. Wearing matching windbreakers.

So I white-knuckled it through my twenties. Blowing it with a series of gals who had waited for me to grow up. A series of gals who got tired and moved on to guys who had already grown up. My sense of self-preservation, or selfishness, had left me single well into my thirties.

What was the point, anyway? All our parents divorced. Why wouldn't we? And the people around me who had married young had started to crack. So I should have counted myself lucky. But I didn't feel that way.

When I looked up, I felt like I had missed it. I was thirty-five. I knew I would never marry. Never have children.

This was my story: I would be an elegant older gentleman. Alone but not lonely. There were other things in life ahead of me. There was charity work. Yes, I would give back the love I had not been given. I would read. Not just horoscopes or magazines, but books. I would garden. Yes, I would fire my gardener. And travel. (If I travelled a lot, I might hire my gardener back—to be determined.) Yes, I would travel! And not just to all-inclusive resorts where I had to wear a brightly coloured wristband, but to Europe. Old cities, where people spoke languages I didn't understand. Yet. But I would learn all the earth's languages. What are there, ten? I would become "polyglot"—a silly word that would come up in many of the interesting conversations I would soon have. I'd often eat in cafés, where waiters would say, *"Sei un signore elegante che è solo ma non solitario."* (Which is Italian for

"You're an elegant gentleman who's alone but not lonely." In case you ever need to know it.)

But it kept coming back to me, like a bad smell that I craved: marriage and children. And tonight, I had blurted it out for the first time.

After Radiohead did a begrudging encore, the Unimpressed Girl and I got into the car.

I said, "Hey, that was fun. Do you want to go somewhere else? A nightcap?"

She thought for a moment and yawned. Yes, yawned. The night was young, but I was old.

Then she said, "You know what I'd really like? To go to the store. I need some bread for the morning."

Sure, why not? That would be a perfect ending to this shitty night.

The last portion of our date was me waiting outside 7-Eleven as she bought a loaf of bread. As Radiohead would have said, I did it to myself.

It was the end of the night. Before she got out of my car, I stammered on about how I "must seem weird, but I'm not. Well, I *am* weird, but not that weird!" She stared at me. And then I said if she wanted "to do something sometime, somewhere, somewhen, give me a dingle." Yes, I used the word "dingle."

The night had been a disaster, and I knew I was letting a summer peach out of my car, and a long winter would follow.

As she got out, I went to give her a peck that I hoped conveyed "Oh well, we tried" more than "I'm creepy." But she turned her head and I caught her in the ear. Not the soft landing I had imagined. She actually wiped her ear before she exited into the safety of the dark night.

Her pretty legs chopped up the sidewalk to her house.

"What a fuck I am," I said to my empty car.

I regrouped for a minute, but then realized that, in her haste to get out, she'd forgotten her bread. What to do? Leave bad enough alone? No, I was now an elegant older gentleman and I would rescue the lady's loaf.

I walked up to the massive Victorian house that had been broken up into starter apartments. I didn't know exactly where she lived. I stared at the faded names and numbers on the intercom. No help.

So I decided to walk around the periphery of the house and maybe find her. Somehow. And as I moved around, huffing and puffing, fate smiled upon me. I heard music. Yes, Radiohead. It was coming from a basement apartment.

I bent down and peered inside. From this precarious angle, I could see a sliver of the apartment. Judging by the decor, it could be her place. But I wanted to make sure. So I pushed my face against the window to get a better look.

Then I saw her.

She was coming out of the bedroom. Of course, after a bad date, all you want to do is get your bad-date clothes off as quickly as possible. Problem was, she hadn't put any clothes back on. She was naked. Then she saw me, leering into—and fogging up—her window. Seemingly (definitely) staring at her tits. She screamed.

I shook the loaf, shouting, "Your bread!" as if that explained everything.

She covered up and yelled, "Just leave it!"

"Where?" I asked.

"Just leave it there! Outside. Anywhere. I'll get it later."

Trying to hold onto my last shred of dignity, I said, "Okay. Call me!" Then I placed the loaf of bread on the snowy ground and went home.

But of course she did not call the next day. She did not call the day after. And no, she did not call the day after that. Or the day after that. Nor did she call the day after the day after that.

But then . . . she called.

We laughed about what she described as "the worst date in history."

"No, I can prove you wrong. I can show you an even worse date."

And she let me. But it wasn't.

This time, I did not ask her about marriage and children. Nor did I see her naked, accidentally or otherwise. And this is the true story that my Pretty Wife and I will one day tell our children of how we met . . .

One evening at sunset, some years later, when we were first living in our Hollywood home, she looked up and I was outside. Wearing a suit and tie, fogging up the window. I had a loaf of bread in my hand and a ring in my pocket. As always, she was way ahead of me.

"Finally!" she said. "What took you so long?"

# One Good Cup

Like running shoes,

The body wears out

From the inside.

The body worn thin by the heart

That pumps too much blood,

Too often,

For all the wrong reasons.


You shouldn't think about things

That you shouldn't think about.

And you definitely shouldn't

Count on what little you know.

Like shoes, head and heart,

It too will wear out.

All I know

Is just enough to fill a thimble.

If you pause here for a night,

You can throw it back

Like a jolt of espresso

And move on.


All I want is one.

One good cup.

One good cup of the bitter brown stuff.


All I want is one.

One gal,

One pal,

One good shirt

That lets the air through.


How many good cups can one man expect

His life to muster?

One.

All I want is one.

One sweet thing

Loading them into

The minivan, or whatnot.


One head on my chest,

One heart,

One breath,

One horoscope to read aloud.

One set of hands to memorize.


All I want is one good cup,

And just enough

To know that one

Is enough.

# Sex Weekend

When you are told to go on a sex weekend, you shouldn't have to be told twice. I think the phrase my Pretty Wife used was "romantic getaway," but we all know that means "sex weekend." It gets hard for couples who have been together a long time, but you've got to keep trying. And I say that because I've learned the hard way—"the hard way" meaning the couples therapist's couch.

I sat in that indent where a thousand sad-asses had sat before me. All us guys learning to "listen better." What I learned is: seduction is not sharing deodorant. Or taking off your own socks. Foreplay is not turning off the TV. Or saying, "Wanna do something? So, then, who should start?" Foreplay is not spitting on your hand.

We're a good couple. But far from perfect. We aren't boastful, like the athlete who spikes the ball when he scores, looks into camera and taunts, "Yeeahhhh! We are happy!" I have noticed that people who have perfect marriages often end up having perfect divorces. So we have kept our heads down, taking quiet notice of the couples that, sadly, didn't make it.

Those of you blessed and/or cursed with a family know that a family is a big, lurching boat. It was for us. But one day, we looked up and realized we were in two boats. Both going the same direction, each paddling as hard as the other. But we were now in two boats.

Kids can be hard on you. You can start impersonating yourself. Weird words begin to emanate from your body. You realize it is the voice of your father. Or mother.

I know a lot of men. Good guys, mostly, who, despite trying their best, haven't made it last. Men who once lived in houses, now living in apartments. The kids they once cuddled, they now call to say goodnight to.

My wife and I had felt cracks. We didn't want the cracks to become crevices, so we went to couples therapy. We realized we'd lost each other a little bit and decided a romantic getaway was a good idea.

But the trip had been bumpy from the start. We got into the room and, well, it wasn't great. For example, the fireplace—it was electric. I mean, I suppose, technically, someone could say, "We cuddled by the roaring electric fire." But not likely.

We all want the same things. To love and be loved in relatively equal amounts. They say "great minds think alike," but in truth, so do bargain hunters. We all want that great room with the view, but not to have to pay so much for it that we can't enjoy being in it.

No, said the bellhop, we were in the junior suite we had paid for.

Anyone who has done any budget romance travel can you tell you, there is a big difference between a suite and a junior suite. Perhaps comparable to the difference between Frank Sinatra and Frank Sinatra, Jr.

The other thing that had thrown the sex weekend off stride was the Young Woman at the front desk. As we were checking in, she smiled at my Pretty Wife and said, "Congratulations." First, there was confusion.

"No, it's not our anniversary," my wife said weakly.

Then that terrible vortex of awkward glances.

The Young Woman had mistaken my wife for pregnant.

"Not now," I thought. "We are on a sex weekend. Or *were*."

No, my wife was not pregnant. Roscoe was one year old at the time and my wife was still breast-feeding. In truth, she had been carrying some baby weight that, she feared, was turning into toddler weight.

This had happened before. In yoga: "Gonna find out the sex of the baby?" At a farmers' market. Her Fish Guy: "Yes, this fish is safe for pregnant women."

And who has to pick up the pieces? Me. By the way, the only time anyone should ever say congratulations to a woman is at her actual baby shower.

"Maybe it's the way you were standing?" I offered helplessly.

My Pretty Wife glared. Not the right thing for me to have said. I know that now.

By the time we got into the room, I was anxious to settle in. And by "settle in," I mean have a drink. Luckily, the ice machine was just around the corner. Unluckily, I knew this because I could hear it from our room—the reassuring hum, the occasional cough of a new batch being released.

In our junior suite, the bumps continued when my wife realized she'd forgotten her breast pump.

"Why can't you find it?" I asked. "Aren't you Nancy Drew?"

She was not in the mood for a joke. Nope, she had forgotten her breast pump and I was going to have to extract the milk the old-fashioned way: using my mouth and, in this instance, a Styrofoam coffee cup. This wasn't even as sexy as it sounds. There was tension in the air.

I got to work on my wife's angry breasts, almost engorged by now. It wasn't bad for the first minute or so, which I think is a personal best. For me, this activity has always been like Hawaiian music. I really like it, but a little goes a long way. It became tough slogging through tense fog. I was confused as to whether I was allowed to enjoy it or not. Apparently, I was doing it all wrong. My face got numb. It was more like erotic assembly-line work.

I was just finding my rhythm—and, in fact, humming "We Will Rock You" in my head as silent motivation—when there was a knock at the door.

It was a Spanish bellhop with a tray. A half-bottle of champagne. Is it pricky to point out it was only a half-bottle? It was from the apologetic Young Woman at the front desk, who, it seems was half-sorry for buzz-killing our sexweekend.

"Compliments of the house."

He went to uncork the champagne by twisting off the top. My wife motioned for him to stop, meaning, "We can do it ourselves. Thanks." Which he took as meaning she didn't want any. And why would a woman in a celebratory junior suite, on the precipice of a romantic weekend, not want any alcohol? Exactly. Preggers.

I could see it on his face. So as he went to form his next sentence, instinctively I leapt up and pointed to the bed.

I don't know why I did that. It's just what I did.

I pointed at the bed, perhaps to say, "Put the tray there." And as I leapt up and pointed at the bed, my white robe—my slightly-too-small-because-we-were-in-an-increasingly-shitty-hotel white robe—popped open. My robe popped open. I pointed at the bed. He thought it was threesome time. Probably common, as he was quite handsome. But not *too* handsome. Just the kind of guy you would want to book for a threesome. Or perhaps he thought I wanted him to have a "go" at my Pretty Wife while I sat, watched and chewed ice? Or took notes, because I'm a writer? I wondered what the Spanish word for "cuckold" was.

(I looked it up later. It is *el cuckedo,* in case you ever need to know it. And while I was at it, *cinta sexo* is "sex tape.")

"No, no, my friend. Nothing like that!"

But in retrospect, he could have been helpful on the milk line.

After he left, my wife turned to me and said sweetly, "Do you think he thought I was pregnant?"

"Of course not! He was flustered because of how sexy you are. And clearly, we are on a romantic getaway."

She bought it, and disappeared into the bathroom. I waited in bed, as is my style. Even a clod knew it was now time for the sex part of the sex weekend.

In the bathroom, I could hear her gargle. Sexy . . .

Now, I am going to get dirty for a minute, but in truth, not as dirty as I'm going to get in two minutes. Okay?

So, my wife came out and opened her white robe to reveal a surprise. A DIY "project" she had been working on before we left home. She had shaved something. Yes, *that.*

Perhaps I'm old, but I missed the memo about why girls started shaving "down there." I was off the market when the practice began. But my research indicates that, around the turn the millennium, they were trimmed to look rectangular. Or box-shaped, as it were.

Then, around 2002, the ladies would make them heart-shaped. Nice idea, but apparently hard to maintain.

Then, around 2003–2005 was the "creative period": an arrow pointing to the important part. "Dude, my button is right there. If you can't figure it out, follow the fur." Or some women would just leave a question mark. As if she didn't know what she wanted in bed and you were supposed to figure it out for her. In this era, there were also a lot of "paint samples"—a woman would just leave a tiny, rectangular chip, showing what colour it would be if she coloured in the whole thing.

Then, in 2008, the whole enchilada. Or taco, as the case may be. And women took it all off and would just walk around whistling. Or at least, that's what I imagine.

But I have to be honest, I don't like it. You've read or skimmed this book: I'm old-fashioned.

I miss the old days, when a woman had a bush and she grew it proudly. Like a farmer growing a cabbage. She watered it and groomed it, sunned it, and if God smiled upon her, the bush would grow. And the bush was good. In my era, I believe there were even "bush-raising bees."

And if you were "down there," tired after a long day, giving your lady a nice "mouth ride," and you sort of dozed off, it'd work nicely as a pillow.

In my day, if you lost your car keys, that was the first place you would look.

The topic had not come up on our first date. The logical question after "How do you feel about marriage and children?" wasn't, "What are your views on the bush?" I guess my Pretty Wife and I had never talked about it. Obviously not, because here she stood.

Then I realized she hadn't done it for her. Of course, she had done it for me. She was trying to "spice things up." A sad phrase I've heard bandied about.

The poor thing, so beautiful. So vulnerable. So often mistaken for pregnant. Standing before me, looking like a plucked chicken. I think I mumbled, "Me likey." We fumbled for a minute. And then—now is the two-minute mark—then she put me on the bed and went down.

At first, I was shocked. Then it was pleasant. I thought, "Hello blowjob, my old friend. You've come to visit me once again." It was warm. Then it began to tingle. Tingle, then burn.

"Ow, ow, ow!"

Remember the gargling I mentioned? Well, I guess this shit show of a hotel offered some alcohol-based menthol moonshine mouthwash that was now kicking up a storm on my dingly dangly. And when I say dangly, I mean it. No man's passion could withstand that.

I ran to the bathroom and put my wilted stem and berries under the cold-water tap.

Bad decision.

It felt like a fire shower of eucalyptuses. My balls retreated back up into my body. It was my own personal "Wreck of the *Edmund Fitzgerald*."

After I stopped crying, that's when she started.

She began to cry and talk. She said she had been trying so hard to make this weekend work, and it felt hopeless. This trip was important because she knew we had to "decide."

"Decide what?" I wondered. Were we breaking up and I didn't even know it? Men are always the last ones to know what is going on in their own lives. That's why we need women. To tell us.

No, she said, we weren't breaking up. But we had to decide if we were going to have another baby. Or not. Before it was too late for us. Apparently, this had been hanging over us and I hadn't even known it. But once she said it, I realized it was true.

From the beginning, we had a tough time deciding to have kids. As it was for many of our best friends, perhaps for you, it could have gone either way. I had always been suspicious of people who had children. Anyone who had kids—and yes, I know, that's a lot of people. I had noticed that when people have kids, it can mute their curiosity and love for the rest of the world. I realize now, after having children, all those people are just exhausted.

I was tired. It had nearly sunk us, and here she was, wondering if I wanted to do it again.

After everything had been said, she went to sleep. It was pitch black. I was rattled, so I followed the groaning beacon to the ice machine. I came back and sat down. Sad and happy.

I sat by the roaring electric fire and looked at my sleeping wife. Would we have another baby? Not a chance. It would crush us like Humpty Dumpty. But we would make it. We were doing our best and we were going to make it. Somehow. I smiled at my gorgeous, engorged wife, asleep. Happy that it would soon be time for my next shift at "the dairy."

# The Bottle Fairy

One of the first fights I ever had with my Pretty Wife was about Santa Claus. I told her I would never tell our future children that Santa Claus existed, because he didn't. How could I lie to our kids? But, of course, in the end, I did.

Our daughter, Heidi, was somehow born with a belief in fairies. Without us even discussing what fairies were, she knew all about them. And my wife nurtured it. She is a scrapbooker at heart, and a frustrated actor. (Aren't they all?) She's the creative type. She read almost half of *The Artist's Way*. So my wife really got into it. She talked to Heidi about all the fairies that seemed to have unlimited time for both of them.

Personally, I think fairies should have jobs. There should be a Warehouse Fairy who flies around, dropping F-bombs and sprinkling overtime. And a Hangover Fairy who takes our hangovers away if we eat "magic food"—bacon. Heidi loved the idea of any fairy, not just the tired Disney crew. But those she loved most were the fairies invented by my wife.

Anybody else out there have a Mail Fairy? We do. His name is Faris (my contribution) and he brings Heidi special mail. A note would read, "Heidi, I was flying by. I love you. Be a good girl and listen to your mom." I believe in fairies as much as the next guy, but isn't that entrapment?

It wasn't long before my wife started to take on the characters of the fairies she and Heidi had imagined. Even more dangerously, she started communicating with Heidi as her various fairy-ish friends.

My particularly obsessive daughter wouldn't go to sleep, so my wife promised that if she did, she'd receive a note in the morning from the Sleep Fairy. I watched in horror as my wife stayed up late and got into character. Rowana, the Sleep Fairy, wrote my daughter a tiny note.

Heidi wrote back. They became friends.

This went on and on. I'd find my wife secretly making fairy paper. She'd look caught, like she'd been cooking meth.

"Don't judge me," she'd say with a wild look in her eyes.

Then we started using these fairies to control our Heidi. To make her behave. And, in fact, to be helpful. "Be helpful" is a nice way of saying "do chores."

"She's going to hate me when she finds out," said my wife.

"Don't worry," I said. "By the time she finds out, she'll be a teenager and she'll hate you anyway."

But still, I too couldn't escape the feeling that we were cheating on our daughter.

Heidi is seven, but she's still a baby at heart. At six, she still drank from a baby bottle. Warm milk at night. "Show and a milk" was her favourite treat. But it became a source of comfort as well as shame for her.

She wouldn't do it in front of her friends. She said she was going to quit, but then she didn't. So we talked about this— my wife the fairy wrangler and myself. Our solution? The Bottle Fairy.

It was like one of those bad heist films. We both vowed, "One more hit and we're out!"

No, the Bottle Fairy doesn't take away your empties so your neighbours won't know what a boozer you are. Apparently, he helps out little shame-filled girls. Raja, the Bottle Fairy, wrote Heidi a note saying how he wanted her to give up her bottles. He needed them for poor kids who didn't have bottles. He would take them to Egypt, Asia and Ireland and give them good homes. We slipped the note under the pillow and waited . . .

The next morning, before dawn, Heidi trundles into our bed, cuddles us for a minute, then says, "I got an interesting letter." She handed the note to my wife, who handed it to me. I did have trouble reading it with my aging eyes, which only helped the subterfuge. I stammered through it, and we all looked at each other. We had a family problem to solve.

Heidi made us get up and show her the places mentioned in the letter on a map. She took in the information and became silent. Which is rare. She went outside and stared up at the morning sky. I turned to my wife and panicked.

"You never should have started this!"

That night, Heidi didn't watch TV. She didn't want a bath. She didn't want a book. And she didn't want her bottle.

Quietly and sadly, she went to bed. Once she was asleep, we composed a new letter, which was all, "We found some bottles in the warehouse, so don't worry about the whole giving-up-the-bottle thing! Signed, Raja." I waited till she was well asleep and tucked it under her pillow. Her beautiful, serious face half-covered in hair. What had we pulled her into? We had wanted her to feel magic, not the adult angst she was now sleeping with.

The next morning, Heidi came in our bed and handed us the letter.

She said, "I don't believe it."

My wife and I just stared at each other.

"I think Raja is just being nice because he can see me and knows I am upset. I want Raja to be proud of me. I'm going to give up my bottles today."

All day, we had heavy hearts as we tried to find loopholes in our fairy plan. After dinner, Heidi started drawing on one of the shoeboxes she collects because my wife collects shoes. We realized she was making a coffin for her bottles. An offering to the fairies.

She decorated the box, and then, like a cop giving up his badge, put the bottles inside. She suggested we put the box into the big tree in the backyard and all say something. We did. Roscoe danced around and babbled, but my wife's and my speeches were more focused and touching.

So, into the branches of our large eucalyptus tree they went.

Afterwards, Heidi said, "I just want to be out here alone for a minute."

I went in to read my son a book. Roscoe could tell I was kind of raw. As I read him *Stinky Socks,* he looked up at me.

"You've read that book before. How come tonight you're crying?"

I said, "Because tonight . . . it's sad."

# Liver

I can tell you firsthand what a shock it is to learn that you have liver cancer. Here's how my medical ordeal unfolded: I'd had a pain in my side. At first, I thought it was from working on my abs. I had been doing sit-ups at my gym, Crunch—ironically, the exercise the club was named for. As I did them, a woman beside me did leg lifts while breaking up with her boyfriend over the phone. From what I could gather, it was his fault. Things he had done. Things he hadn't done. The usual. I remember looking at her—so pretty, so public—and thinking, "My side hurts. I hope it isn't anything strange." And of course, by "strange," I meant "serious."

But the pain went away. I presume the woman and the guy went on to see other people. I have often thought about them, wondering how things turned out. I'm weird that way.

Then, about a week later, you guessed it: the pain came back. This time, it really ached. There was a tender area. I realized it wasn't my abs that were hurting. It was something else. Something deep inside me. How dumb can a smart man be? I have done abs all my life. I've lifted weights. I've won a ribbon (if not the trophy) in wrestling. I have run marathons and even vacuumed and never felt this pain before. There is one thing that an old man does not want to feel, and it's a new pain. As I pushed at the area, it throbbed back. It seemed swollen.

Luckily, I had booked an adjustment with my chiropractor, Heather, for the next day. I told myself not to panic till then. Another great thing about L.A. is no one is just what they are. They are more. My chiropractor also specializes in holistic medicine, energy (whatever that means) and, more presciently, organs. I told Heather about my pain.

"Let's find the source."

The word "source" sort of bugged me. This was getting serious.

"No, it isn't," I told myself. "She is just a chiropractor putting her thumbs on various parts of your body and pushing your arms while closing her eyes."

She opened her eyes and got sombre. "It's coming from your gallbladder or your liver."

I gulped, trying to recall what little I remembered from health class. I should have listened instead of sitting there drawing dragsters. The gallblader is no big deal, right? But I was pretty sure the liver was important. I remember looking at the map of the body on her wall and thinking, "We are all so strong, but we are all so fragile."

Then she did another test. She started pushing on my stomach. And then my back. Searching for tender spots as she went. When she found one particularly "troublesome area," she stopped. Eureka. Instinctively, her hands leapt up away from me. Then she cleared her throat. Okay, now I'm in hell. You can't clear your throat before you give your shirtless patient a prognosis. Am I in a TV movie all of a sudden?

"It's coming from your liver. It could be nothing."

Which really meant, "It could be something. It could be everything."

I asked her what it most likely was.

She responded, "You should have it checked out as soon as possible."

You may have noticed that she didn't answer my question.

On the way home, the red lights were never so long, but when they turned green, I didn't want to go. The universe knew something was up, because on the radio was an ad for "City of Hope," the "best of the best when it comes to cancer treatment." I was trying to remember if liver cancer was one of the "bad" ones. Then a kid's joke popped into my head.

"Of course they call it your liver, because you can't live without it."

I tried to find some hard rock music to wipe the worry away. That is the other thing that's wrong with L.A.: no classic rock. Shouldn't "L.A. Woman" be playing at all times? Perhaps my mind had seized on this scarcity of rock in avoidance. Avoiding what I had just noticed: a slight cough. Just like in the TV movie where the dad is playing baseball with his son and coughs. Four scenes later, he's dead.

Of course, it was happening now. My Pretty Wife and I had had the arrogance to be going through a good patch. One where we quietly admitted to each other that we were happy. We had held hands the night before as we watched the sunset.

How could we? How cliché! How arrogant. How forboding. Who did we think were, holding hands and taunting fate? Of course I was getting struck down for wandering into the land of the happy.

Then an old joke of mine entered my mind: "Do you know the difference between an optimist and a pessimist? An optimist says, 'The glass is half full.' A pessimist says, 'The glass is half full, but I probably have bowel cancer.'"

Or liver cancer?

I went home. I snuck up into my office and Googled "liver pain." Up popped "liver cancer pain." I quietly closed the door. I panicked and I surfed. I couldn't find anything that wasn't about cancer or bone marrow.

"Cancer. Oh, cancer is sad," I recalled a troupemate saying in a sketch, seemingly from a previous life. The sickly truth was, I had had a drink or two in my long life.

Later, my Pretty Wife came home, so beautiful, so innocent as she put down the blood oranges she had bought. Blood oranges, not to be confused with the regular ones that hung in the tree outside. I thought, "This is her face, quiet and beautiful. This is her face before she knows. Now I have to change that pretty face forever."

I pulled her into the bedroom—and not the way they do in erotic fiction. She's a tough woman. She can take the worst news with a simple cock of her head and say, "Huh." I started gushing details. She calmed me down.

She looked into the middle distance and said, "I'm sure it's nothing. You should talk to Heather about it. She's a genius when it comes to this kind of thing."

I told her that I'd already seen Heather.

"What did she say?" asked my Pretty Concerned Wife.

"She didn't. She told me to see a doctor as soon as humanly possible."

She buckled, but did not break. We locked eyes, our fear ricocheting off of each other. So . . . here we were.

That night, as I lay there, trying to sleep, she quietly got up and snuck on her computer. In the distance, I could hear her sigh and whimper as she read all the same stuff I had read. And more—the woman is thorough. As she finally returned to bed, I pretended I was asleep.

I phoned my doctor's office first thing in the morning. They told me he was in surgery that day and couldn't see me. I persisted. I told them it was a matter of "great urgency."

"An emergency?"

"And then some."

They squeezed me in. The nurse took my blood for a series of tests without telling me much.

That evening, the phone rang. We fumbled for it, but it went to voicemail. It was my doctor telling me he had some concerns about my blood work and wanted to see me the next day . . .

I felt like a jihadist sitting in the explosive vest, waiting. "Tomorrow," I thought, "I will see the doctor. Tomorrow, the next part will begin. Tomorrow."

The cough continued. If this were the TV movie, there would be lilting flute music.

We were in free fall. In bed, we lay together in our separate hells. I was wet with sweat. She kept sucking her teeth. We couldn't hold each other because we knew we if we came together we would fall apart. At one point, though, my wife muttered, "I have a student loan." Which I later learned was actually, "I can't do it alone." We lay thinking about my last days on earth and hers as a widow soon to begin. We'd previously had a running joke that my last words would be "Don't remarr—" which she would mistake for "Don't remodel." And of course, without the comforting activity of remodelling, she would go out and meet a guy and, eventually, remarry.

But now, as I lay there in the dark, I wanted her to find someone. Someday. Soon. Her life must go on. But with whom? One of my friends who had always lurked in the shadows? The guy we referred to quite descriptively as Pillow Lips? The Cheese Guy from the farmers' market?

As a lifelong comedian, I wondered if, after I died, I should leave my brain to science, so they could study it for the effects of "repetitive bombing." There is very little research being done in that area, and I think I would be a good specimen.

What about my kids? I had to wake up my children right now and teach them the spaghetti recipe I had inherited from my father (here's the secret: use cinnamon). I had to download all I knew before it was too late. Before the new husband moved in and started playing all his goddamn jazz music. Or world beat. I think my Roscoe would be okay—I had brainwashed him with rock. But Heidi? She could let her ears get hijacked if Pretty Widow chose the wrong lunk. I would have to get up and make a mixed tape. Or ten. Before time ran out. And of course, music was just the tip of the iceberg.

I got up and wandered around the house, not turning off lights, but rather, putting them on for comfort. I wondered what things she would sell when she remodelled. Then I started writing all the smart things I knew for my kids to read later. What do I call it? *Advice to My Children in the Case of My Death, Which Seems Imminent*?

No, change "imminent" to "possible." Don't want to scare them.

Well, they'd know I was dead by the time they were reading it, no? Christ, I can't even think of a title.

Should I wake up Roscoe and see if he has a title? He's a genius with titles. He *did* think up the name of this book. No. Let the kids sleep. Just brainstorm: *Walk Placidly Amidst the Haste*. Shit, that's the Desiderata! The seventies hippy poem that hung on everyone's wall. I don't believe in it. In fact, *don't* walk placidly amidst the haste. If you do, people will think you are stupid. Or a Christian. *Be Nice, but Not Too Nice*. Now, that's better . . . So I worked as long as I could on this. The shards of knowledge I thought I'd learned. The advice I wish someone had given me.

I can never sleep, but that night was especially bad.

When you are up between 3 and 4 a.m., know I am awake too. Every night. Like a reverse nap, I open my eyes for a short while. Nightly, my brain wakes me up to think my thoughts. Counting troubles and blessings. Listening to the mysterious sounds the house makes when we are not looking . . .

•••

All my life, when I haven't been able to sleep, I have played mental games of my own creation. I imagine my bed floating up and out of my house. Steering my bed, I begin to fly. I move through the sky. Down the hill past the Viper Room I go. Sometimes I stop there to see if I am on the guest list. But usually not.

I flutter over streets lined with discarded furniture by day. At night, that furniture is gone. It's probably somewhere safe and warm now. It found someone, or someone found it.

When I am feeling generous or lost, I sail past my friends' places, checking on them to make sure they are okay. When all is safe, I imagine gliding out of the city to where it's quiet.

Suburbs melt into farms. Gaining speed, I move out over the prairies.

If I am not asleep yet, I dive down towards the lights that twinkle from the meth labs below. I hover there and whisper to the troubled souls inside.

"Buddy, I think it's time to go to sleep. You'll be okay. I know you will."

Then, on I go.

Arrogant as it sounds, I imagine "fixing" people as I travel. I float to Canada. The land I am from. Checking on strangers and stragglers along the way.

We are all so alone. Especially at night.

But so connected. Especially at night.

In my twenties, I thought about what the world could give to me. In my thirties, what the world thought of me. In my forties, what I thought of the world. I think the world is a place as savage as it is beautiful. A place as happy as it is sad. As we get older, competition and cynicism leave us. What replaces them, hopefully, is humanity. In the moment I realized that I loved the world, I also knew I would soon be leaving it . . .

The next day, my Pretty Wife and I went to the doctor to confirm what we already knew. I was living with liver cancer. We needed to bravely consider the options and hope we were talking in terms of years, not months. Months, not weeks. We waited in the type of brightly lit room that would one day demarcate all our lives. Before and after.

The doctor walked in, looked at me and smiled. Then noticed

my wife was there too. When he said "Hello," my wife and I both broke down crying. Not just crying, but blubbering. Snot flying out of our noses, the whole deal.

The doctor asked what was wrong. I looked at him, trying to be calm. I didn't want him to be too upset. I was suddenly kind, now that I was dying.

"I have liver cancer. We think."

"No," said my Pretty Wife. "We're fairly sure."

He started probing me and asking me a bunch of weird questions about my diet. I braced myself for him to tell me that I possessed a liquor-shrivelled liver that resembled a fortune cookie—and the fortune inside read, "You die."

"What do the tests show? What's happening in my blood?"

He cleared his throat. Yes, cleared his throat. We were living in a TV movie, don't forget.

"Well, your cholesterol's high. We need to put you on something."

"What about my liver cancer?"

"Liver cancer? None of the symptoms of liver cancer would manifest like what you are describing. If you had liver cancer, you wouldn't even know it.

"Wait," I said. "So I *might* have liver cancer and not know it?"

"No, you don't have liver cancer."

"But I *could* have it?"

"No, you don't! Your health risk is—you're getting fat!"

My wife and I looked at each other and did what we had never done before or since: we high-fived. What great news, I was going to live. I was just really fat!

# The "Brucie-Derata"

You are a child not of the universe, but of your parents.

You have the right to outwit, outplay and outlast them.

It is the basis of evolution.


Don't walk placidly amidst the haste. People will think you are

stupid.

Or a Christian.


As far as possible, be nice. But not too nice.

Because you'll be labelled as "just really nice."

Then you'll have to be nice all the time.

It will be a jail of your own creation.

When you are young, do not trust people just because they are old.

When you get older, do not trust people just because they are young.

Our mistakes make us who we are.

Our accomplishments who we *think* we are.

Only time will reveal which are which.

If you have to burn your bridges, make sure you cross them first.

You can date a "crazy chick," but do not marry one.

You can date a "bad boy," but you cannot change him.

Always know you are responsible for your own mood.

Even if lesser fools put you in a bad mood.

If you forget someone's name, it's not your fault.

It's theirs for not being more memorable.

Therefore, on this earth, dullards should wear nametags.

Don't rush to become who you are.

It might take you longer to get there if you do.

Follow your dream.

Unless your dream is exactly the same as everybody else's dream.

Like "become a star."

Or merely "be famous."

In those cases, don't follow your dreams.

Get a job.

Never ask a question you don't want the answer to.

For example, "Are you happy?"

Or "Do you like my red glasses?"

The pornography we make as an act of freedom in our youth can become shackles of shame in our old age.

So be careful with the camcorder.

Don't be creepy in bed.

But then again, one person's "creepy" is another person's "wild."

So proceed cautiously between the sheets.

The secret to happiness is this: set the coffeemaker at night.

So when you get up, the coffee's ready!

Perhaps that's not the secret to happiness, but more of a helpful hint.

Regarding karma, those people who you think will "get theirs," won't.

They will keep using yours.

The quicker you come to peace with this, the happier you will be.

Remember, the love you are given will pour right through you if you don't know who you are.

Cry when you have to. Otherwise, the tear you don't cry will, one day, become a wave.

Life is a beautiful miracle that rises up from the universe to flow through you.

But life can also be really boring too.

So turn to each other to help you through this dull, beautiful life . . .

# Forty-One Steps

There are forty-one steps from the street up to the theatre space where most of my skit troupe sit waiting. How do I know the exact number of steps? By counting each one as it echoes through the poster-filled stairway.

*Boom.* Then a long pause. A long, long pause.

Then, *boom.* That's two. When the echoing man finally arrives, he looks like George Burns in *Oh God! III*.

You may not remember *Oh God! III*—only the laugh-filled original and the heartfelt sequel. Because *Oh God! III* never got made. Burns passed away the first day of filming. The crew thought he was doing the longest deadpan of all time. And in a way, he was. He was dead.

I believe they shot a few scenes with George Burns's cigar and toupee, but it wasn't working, so the project was shelved.

I tell you this to indicate that the guy we've been waiting for doesn't look so good. But he is the Showman of the group. He, whose steps have slowly echoed up, has always been so light on his feet. In so much of a hurry. Busting to tell you a story. But now, this once billowing soundscape seems more like Sankai Juku, the Buddhist performance-art troupe, than a guy making a pithy comedy entrance.

Here's why: the Showman is now the Sick One.

He finally makes it to the top of the stairs and has to sit down for a minute. Catch what's left of his breath. We try not to give him too much—or too little—attention.

"Sorry I'm late."

The rest of us look around, sharing worried glances, "Wow. He must really be sick. He hasn't apologized in twenty years." None of us has. It's part of our unspoken language: never be wrong. And when you are, don't apologize for it.

So the five of us sit, the old married couple that we are, waiting for someone (we've never been sure who) to tell us to begin.

The Serious One reads his newspaper, as always. He mutters to no one in particular, "Oh look. Farrah Fawcett just died."

I watch the words come out of his mouth, move across the table, do a double take and look right at the Sick One. It is one of those things that is exactly the wrong thing to say. That's why the brain does it, I think. Once he realizes he has said it, the Serious One wants his words back. Too late. The words hit the Sick One like a grenade.

"I'm gonna die too, aren't I?"

No. Of course not. "Why would a man with cancer die?" says the once-boyish Quippy One.

There is a gallows laugh. One of a million over the years. So we turn to our scripts and start reading.

The cruel coincidence is that we are reading our most recent mini-series, called *Death Comes to Town*. The Sick One insists that we change the title. We all know why. We try to come up with alternatives: *Demise-ville*; *The Opposite of Life . . . Town*; *The Grim-Keepers*; and the worst, *Mini-Serious*. Nah.

We have decided early on to not let him win a comedy argument "just because he had cancer." Tough group. So we keep the title as *Death Comes to Town*. And it feels like maybe it has.

The Sick One gets up from the table. He doesn't do what he usually does, which is go over to the craft table and touch every sandwich, playing them like they're bongos, before eating only six. He goes and lies down on a futon in the corner.

Everyone looks at me. "Do something." The elephant in the room is that I played Cancer Boy in our both under- and overappreciated film, *Brain Candy*. A character I fought for and insisted stay in the film, despite people's protests.

Cancer Boy prompted hate mail: "You should all get cancer and die."

Perhaps, as far as karma was concerned, it's my fault.

I look over to the futon and notice that the Showman's back is moving. I can't see his face, but he's either laughing or crying. I don't think he's laughing.

So I go and lie down next to him and tell him he's not going to die, even though I have no actual information on the topic. In fact, although it looks to the contrary, I say he's going to be the last of us standing.

Then we start riffing about how the rest of the troupe are going to die. This idea intrigues him. In this family, it's always ideas that bring people back from the brink.

"How?" he asks.

"Well, the Curly-Haired, Funny One is going to apologize to death. One day, his heart will give out in the middle of 'I'm sor—' 'I'm sore?'"

Terrible joke, but he laughs anyway. I proceed. "The Quippy

One will die of either a ferret or a snake bite at some after-after-after party in a bad part of town. That he confused for the good part of town because he'd had a few drinks."

He gives a slight chuckle, then says, "Of course, Bruce, you will die of cancer, not me. You'll get it to copy me, but then take it too far. As you always do."

"The Serious One? Let's see . . . he'll be killed by a waiter."

"No," says my futon-mate, "a sommelier. He'll be murdered for sending back so many bottles of wine."

We share a light laugh.

"And the bottle he's killed with? He'll send that back too."

And then we just lie there, praying.

Whom do you pray to when you have no God? Who is the God of the Godless? But if, right now, God warbled the *Kids in the Hall* theme song ominously, we would believe in him. Finally realizing he exists, because he's funny. To us, anyone who isn't funny doesn't exist.


This is not the first time I lie with the Showman when he is down. This isn't the first time he has played hurt. It had happened before, a few years earlier. The last time we were all on tour. We were playing San Francisco. The theatre was huge—in fact, there was a big vom in front of the stage. So the first row of seats was, like, a hundred yards back and it was driving us crazy. Especially him. Anything that drives anyone crazy always drives him crazier.

Anyway, for the encore of our San Fran show, the Head Crusher made fun of our careers and crushed our heads.

"Oh, I have two words for you, Poker Show. I'm crushing your head!"

Really cutting-edge material.

With the Showman, the Head Crusher busts him for always going too far. And it's true. I love him, but sometimes he's like a restaurant that isn't so sure about the quality of the food, so they give you really big portions, you know?

So when the Head Crusher crushed the Showman's head, he didn't lie down on the stage. Which is what we always did. Instead, he jumped off the stage. Why? I have no idea. To be closer to "the people"? To prove he could be a really old punk?

He jumped into the vom.

The vom was deep. It was dark. It echoed, and I thought I could smell moss. He jumped off into this void, and there was a moment where we all watched him. A little bit like Wile E. Coyote, he hung there for a second, and then was gone.

We waited for what seemed like a long time, and from the darkness, we heard, "Ugh . . . oh my God. I swallowed my contact lens!"

Being professionals, we all giggled, but continued.

Somehow, he made it back on stage. He didn't look good. As we bowed, he did something he'd never done before. He didn't bow. Now, we knew something was really wrong. He couldn't bend. So he bowed with his face.

Then he muttered to me, "I'm very hurt."

An ambulance was called. I'll never forget hearing over the walkie-talkies, "We have a middle-aged white male with lower back trauma." So I, being the dad of the group and the only one who ever had a credit card on him, went with him to the hospital. The hospital was, like, a block away, but the ride still cost $1,900. Modern medicine.

We got to the hospital. It was in the middle of the Tenderloin district and it was Saturday night, so it was a zoo. We met some kindly "cray-cray" people. I met a few people with broken collarbones and other injuries who insisted they were the mayor.

"You can't *all* be the mayor."

Turned out the Showman was fine, so they released him. But

my favourite part was at the end, when he said, "It's all good. I don't think anybody recognized me."

"No, 'cause you're not a crack dealer."

And for the rest of the tour, the rest of us, being so kind, teased, "We have a middle-aged white male with lower back trauma."


So, while we're lying on the terrible futon, one of the guys must have remembered this story. Because we hear, "We have a middle-aged white male with lower back trauma. Could be cancer. Could be he's faking for sympathy." Everyone laughs. He gets up. We somehow get back to work.

We finish rehearsal and then the mini-series.

Years later, Scott is fine. Fitter and funnier than ever. In fact, he kicked cancer's ass.

"Stay down, cancer!" I'm sure he taunted, as he told the long, funny story.

The Sick One is now the Showman, once again.

# *Taco Bell*

My dad died recently, but do the people at Taco Bell care? Perhaps I am getting ahead of myself. My dad had been, in his life, a very loud introvert. He was a man with the gift of gab. Rants, lectures, dirty jokes he had already told you. So it was quite sad that he got ALS and slowly lost the "gift" of speech. Or as Alanis Morissette might have called it, had she been standing in that cruelly lit Edmonton hospital, ironic.

But we sat there, day after day, slowly feeding him apple-sauce. He ate about a spoonful an hour. Perhaps you've been on applesauce detail and know the drill. I recall looking deep inside his mouth, for perhaps the last time, and thinking,

"Remember it, Bruce. Remember the inside of your daddy's mouth. This could be your last chance." As I did, I noticed the gold in his back teeth.

I thought, "We are not burying him with those still in his head. Are we? The waste would kill him again."

I took a break. All that sluggish applesauce feeding had put a kink in my neck. I walked downstairs. I surveyed the small, concerned groups. They all loved their people too and were as lost and tired as I was. As the sun hit my forearms and the Tim Hortons coffee hit my lips, I had a simple obvious thought: life is pretty cool. Even these, even the "dying days," are beautiful.

Back upstairs, it was all over. My dad had gone. It was like watching a really long, terrible movie, but still being disappointed that you missed the obvious ending.

Truthfully, I wasn't even one bit sad. When I looked down at dead Dad, I felt nothing. The first thought that hit me (truly) was, "I never saw Johnny Cash play." Weird, huh? Perhaps not so weird if you ever had the occasion to see Johnny Cash play. Now I'll never know.

Beside Dad lay the clipboard he used to write his notes and "directives" on. I deciphered the chicken scratch as a joke he was trying to tell the nurse. My dad died in the middle of a joke? I was horrified. I would never do that. I would have the performer's instinct to finish. Then go.

(Parenthetically, as a lifelong runner I have often hoped that the last thing I would do before I died is press my stopwatch. You know, to get my time.)

His memorial service was not a well-attended affair. It was not sold out. There were six people. Including him. That is what happens when you hole up in a trailer and your only friends are a coffee cup and a cigarette pack. That's what happens when you lock the doors and close the windows—presumably so you don't waste any of the cigarette smoke.

The good news was that at his service, I had a great set. I improvised the above stopwatch joke and a bit about the inventor of Gatorade—who, as it turned out, had also recently died. I theorized that, as the seconds wound down in his life, the doctors probably snuck up behind him with a cooler of Gatorade and poured it on his rich, dying head.

"He started it," I quipped. *Boom*. Big laugh.

Wow, my dad had died and now I was having the best set of my life!

"My dad should die more often," I thought.

After his service, it was time to go and spread his ashes. I won't say too much about the specifics of this, as I don't want the good people at Safeway to get upset, but there are times when being known as a comedian can be helpful. One of those times is when you get caught emptying your dad's ashes into a Safeway dumpster. Because, when you are asked what you're doing, if you say, "Oh, just releasing my dad's ashes into this dumpster," the person who caught you doing it will laugh.

Not knowing what to do after the service, it seemed logical to go to a Taco Bell. Grief logic. Maybe that's what they are there for. Inside, something came over me. I went up to the counter and said, "Hi, my dad has just died, so can I have some free food?"

The guy just stared at me. He was one of those young fools with his whole life ahead of him. You know the type. He just shrugged no. I glanced at his nametag to use his name—a trick I had learned from my dead salesman father. His nametag read "Nametag." It's ironic, he explained.

"Nametag, I used to be you. I used to have a shirt named Ricky. When I worked at Canada Dry."

He just stared at me.

"So, Nametag, my dad just died, so can I have a free Burrito Supreme and a small drink?"

"No."

"No?! Listen, no one came to his funeral because he was a prick. Nametag, don't be a prick. No one will come to your funeral. Cough up some Churros."

Blank stare.

So I made my well-timed exit. Meaning, security dragged me out. And as they did, I grabbed a single shard of ice from the drink fountain. A symbolic solo piece. I mean, we all die alone, but some of us *really* die alone. I chewed that ice down. When I did, something happened to me. As the ice flowed into my body, I finally got sad. Sad, then happy. Because I got him back.

Many of you may know what it's like to struggle with a declining pet or a parent. How you can only see them in terms of the terrible end. But the good news is, when they are gone, you get them back. Not just the tough last part, but the whole life. The man who had played "Hibernation" with me. The guy who played Yahtzee with me. And cheated. The strong young man who stormed into my room to demand I turn down *Quadrophenia*. And then stayed and listened. I put the piece of ice in my mouth and it melted into me. Flowed into me, where he will remain.

The only thing I remember from school is: air never ages and it's never destroyed. I just love that idea. So when you think about it, we are breathing the same air as all the people who walked before us. Kafka. Joe Strummer. Your grandparents. All the people. All the pets. All those you have loved and lost, or simply "blown it" with, are there. In the air. And if you miss them, just take a breath . . .

# Dad as Dog

When I was a kid, Halloween was going through a "bad patch." There were razor blades reported in apples. No one ever saw one, but there were "reports."

The candy—don't get me started—was made of lard and molasses. It was so tough it could take a bullet. The ghostly wax-paper wrappers always fused with the candy, but you'd gnaw on it anyway. The widower on the corner gave out caramel corn, but you'd have to sing a song. What a morose "festive" night.

Back then, you couldn't buy Halloween costumes in stores, so your mom would have to sew one by hand (not happening in our home). Or you'd have to make do. A lot of guys on the hockey team went as hockey players. Or you'd wear your dad's old clothes and go out as a hobo.

Unhappy families are the most unhappy when they're measured against happy ones. When what's supposed to be a happy family time isn't. So, like many of you who grew up in "challenging" or "flawed" homes, my wife and I vowed something different for our kids. For them, there would be no half-cooked turkeys hurled at the wall. No Christmas trees pushed over to make a point. And Halloween would be "spooky" and "haunting," but not because of us.

Halloween was a happy time for the family the first few years. I went out as Robin to my son's Batman. Then he and I went as Hall and Oates. My wife went as a Picasso painting, then dressed as the year 1960. She's artsy that way.

My daughter, Heidi, went as a few princesses. But then she didn't want to be part of the "princess army" anymore. She craved to be more original. But what?

She became obsessed, searching through the stacks of catalogues that were shovelled into our mailbox. We were on the "too much disposable income for their own good" mailing list. Heidi would devour the pages of these catalogues, cooing, circling her favourites. Impractical things with wings. People who want your money think of everything, and these catalogues even create their own characters. I know zombies don't exist, but "candy-corn families" and "futuristic chimney sweeps" *really* don't exist.

What's worse, she wanted us all to go out as a family. I was tempted to veto her dreams, which I thought would be good practice for when she got older. But I couldn't. We were happy.

But last year, as Halloween rolled around, there was trouble in the air. Our family pet, Lulu, a white standard poodle, was not doing well. She had a nosebleed that had started quietly enough, but was now gaining momentum.

The bleeding would not stop.

We'd walk Lulu to the park—and, using the trail, we could find our way back home.

"Is this normal?" Roscoe asked.

I told him we lived in a world so crazy that everything was normal. He didn't buy it. He turned inward and started punishing his Legos. Wearing a cardboard Minecraft head while he watched TV. And I turned into my dad—pretending things were okay, hoping they would be later.

For anyone who has ever had to wrap a pet in a blanket and rush it into a pet hospital, I will spare you the gruesome details.

But three worst-case pieces of news and two operations later, we were on tenterhooks.

One afternoon, my wife and I were picking up Heidi and Roscoe from karate class. The kids were lethargic from the stress in the house and their disdain for karate. Then we got "the call."

"Get here fast."

Lulu was in trouble. We tried to race there without the kids knowing what was up, but Heidi asked, "Dad, why are you racing?"

"Can you believe we have to give these people some money before the bank closes?" I stumbled.

Unbelievably, she believed it.

So while the kids waited in the car, my wife and I went in and greeted our glassy-eyed girl. Her tail flinched, but did not wag. She had the impulse, but not the strength. I looked at Lulu and knew that it was all over but the ending. My wife and I had a talk with her, and then—we had to put poor Lulu down.

We held her until we didn't need to anymore. Not exactly a date night, but it was a shared activity nonetheless. It was the hardest thing I've ever done. My dad dying was a nuisance compared to this.

Moments later, as we emerged minus a family member, the kids lost their minds. (In fairness, though, I think there were also blood-sugar issues). I had to explain, "Lulu went to heaven."

I don't believe in heaven, and I'm a terrible actor at the best of times, so the kids just stared. Then lips started to quiver. Roscoe started kicking the back of the seat like a racehorse. You can imagine, or have lived through, the rest. We drove straight to a drive-thru. Happy meals that weren't. My wife, wearing sunglasses and crying while she ate an ice cream cone, babbled, "The calories don't count if your dog just died."

The days that followed were a sad blur. When a parent dies, you're allowed to grieve for a year. When your dog dies, you get the day off work. And you feel guilty too. Why would I grieve more for my dog than my dad? Why would her bowls, blankets and toys seem more precious than his old slippers?

But it was worse for my children.

As Halloween drew nearer, Heidi didn't have any interest. Her teacher gave her a book to help her deal. Unbelievably, it was called *Saying Goodbye to Lulu*. It featured a ragtag dog named Lulu. What are the odds? My wife and I tried our best to read the kids the book. We would tag-team, changing readers when our voices cracked. It took a few nights, but we got through it. For anyone in the market, be warned: this is a work of dark cruelty. The dog dies wrapped in the little girl's favourite sweater and is later buried in the backyard. In a box. With a sock from each family member (for some reason).

But this brought up the obvious for Heidi: that she, like the girl in the book, had not gotten to say goodbye to Lulu.

A few days later, I came home and noticed that the mood in the house had shifted. No longer was there a feeling of loss looming in the air. Had I gotten a job that I didn't know about yet? No. My family was excited because Halloween was on after all. Heidi was going out as some sort of fairy and Roscoe was going as a ninja. Or an owl. The kids had a great idea of what I should be.

"You're going to be Lulu," said Heidi.

As a parent, you get used to being a prop. Your kids dress you any way they see fit. Braid your hair. Paint your toenails. But dad as dog? This was too much.

Nervously, I countered, "You know who would make a great Lulu? Mom. She's more of a traditional actor than I am. She's even done 'mask work.'"

"No way," my wife replied. "I'm going as Frida Kahlo—if she hadn't had the accident. Good, right?"

Like so many things in a dad's life, you just have to bite the inside of your mouth and do it.

What will I say to the neighbours whose names I only know because we've gotten their mail by accident? "Don't mind me, I'm dressed as a family pet that up and died on my kids." Or "It's the darndest thing. Remember that trail of blood 'round the neighbourhood last month?"

My wife instantly had her computer out, looking for dog costumes. But nothing seemed right to the kids, who vetoed one after another. Then I realized I had to return to my childhood. We'd have to make our own. The kids were excited as the costume came together. It was exactly as you'd imagine: a cotton ball–covered off-white tracksuit, a white tuque outfitted with homemade ears. The last morbid detail was a felt collar that held Lulu's actual dog tags.

The other development: we were having a Halloween party so that everyone could come and, well, say goodbye to Lulu. So up went the ghosts and the bouncy castle.

As the hour approached, I outfitted myself for the worst gig of my life. "At least I don't have any lines," I thought. I pulled on the costume, and the grim mission was underway. I became my dead dog.

*Ding dong*. It was go time.

The moment the first two princesses arrived, Heidi wobbled into the kitchen and projectile puked rainbow sludge all over the kitchen island. (My wife and I now laughingly call it Puke Island). "What goes around, comes around" isn't a saying about karma. It's about the stomach flu. Roscoe had had it earlier in the week. We'd been worried that we'd have to cancel the party, but he'd pulled through. But now, Heidi had it.

(Here's a secret: when your child gets sick, you kind of blame the parents at school who don't make as much money as you. And also you start to worry that your child will give it to the kid whose parents make more than you. Maybe that's more about me?)

My wife and I stared at the puke on the floor. Our worst nightmare had come true. What to do? In that moment, I got a flash of what my dad would have done: pretend things are okay so that maybe they would be later.

We sprang into action. My wife threw towels on the floor and I took Heidi into the TV room that, conveniently, still had the dog gate. Like bars to keep us in and people out. While outside, the bouncy house bounced and goblin cookies got gobbled, we sat sequestered.

Outside, my son was busy showing off his "ninja skills," even though he was dressed as an owl, and my wife worked desperately to make the monkey on Frida's shoulder stand up. But I was happily with Heidi, sipping ginger ale and waving to the "visitors" outside the bars.

This is all I ever really wanted a family for. Watching *Little Bear* and cuddling.

And for the first time, Heidi started telling me about what she wanted to be in life. A conversation I never had with my father.

As the party wound down, Heidi made her final farewells. Then she turned to me, stroked my ear, touched my tags and said, "Goodbye, Lulu." My heart both broke and was healed at the same time.

Finally, she had gotten to say it. Someday, she would say it to me.

That night, I woke up with "the feeling" in my throat. As I rushed to the toilet, I caught a glimpse of myself in the mirror, dog paint still smudged on my face. In that instant, it flashed through my brain. I'd made it.

I've had three families in my life. The one I crawled out of as a child. The one I had crawled into—namely, the Kids in the Hall. And this one.

I had survived a crappy family and somehow created better ones. With that, I leaned down into the cold, quiet bowl below me and threw up. Puking, but happy . . .

# They Started the Riot without Me

Written after all the rest. And on a new computer.

My family and I walked into our house. It looked like someone had started the riot without me. All the drawers were torn out. My suit jackets were scattered like Kleenex. The furniture was turned over. Yep. We had been robbed. *Now* it made sense that our mailbox was missing.

The day before, I had just finished my book (yes, this very book) and pressed "send" on my computer and enjoyed the thunderous sound of it whooshing off into the universe. Or so

I imagined. My wife even gave me a little round of applause, with only the slightest hint of sarcasm in it. We sat by the fire: my Pretty Wife, my suddenly charming children and me. You can imagine how good I felt.

My wife had started planning a party to celebrate my achievement. And I was too happy to stop her. We didn't know who to invite, so we stumbled onto the great (terrible) idea of inviting everyone we knew. Why not? It'd been a long time since we'd had everybody over. So I'd forgotten that I don't like having everybody over.

But the next day, we drove down the hill to have a more private family affair—clubhouse sandwiches and fries. Then a robbery for dessert.

We came up the driveway and I thought, "That's weird. Where's my mailbox?" I had the satisfying thought that no mailbox means no catalogue companies trying bait us into buying. But then we realized the front door was open.

How stupid were we? It was our fault. We hadn't set our state-of-the-art alarm system.

Walking into your house after it's been robbed is surreal. Suddenly, it feels strange and new. Things you'd taken for granted and forgotten are now strewn across the floor. You are angry at what they took. And what they didn't take. "Our camera isn't good enough for you? Who do you think you are?"

Heidi looked up at my wife, her eyes full of fear. "Mom, can't you figure out who did this? You're Nancy Drew."

A running joke gone sour.

Heidi rushed to check on her dolls; they were still there. But other stuff was gone. They had taken my computer. All my work, ideas and notes. All I had left were my forty tartan note-books, which had been scraped for ideas over the years. They had taken Roscoe's piggy bank, which had been empty. And Heidi's piggy bank, which had been full. They had even busted open a wooden box that we kept locked beside our bed. They must have thought it contained cocaine, but it didn't. It was Lulu's ashes. They took our dog's ashes, but left the broken box.

I imagined them snorting my dog. My anger grew.

There was a cautious knock at the door. It was our mailman. Mail-lady, actually. She pointed out the obvious: "Your mail-box is gone." She handed us our mail, but not before telling us several horror stories of mail thieves and gangs who will steal anything made of metal.

"Gangs?!" said Roscoe, now horrified.

Later, as we waited for the police, I tried to calm myself by rifling through the mail. There was an envelope that I liked the look of: a residuals cheque for my wife. I handed it to her hopefully. She opened it. It was a cheque for thirty-nine cents. A final blow. She crumbled. "It costs more than that to mail it. Why do they even bother? Why do *I* even bother?" The insulting cheque and the robbery were too much for her. She finally cracked.

"Sure, why not? Rob us, underpay us and snort our dog's ashes! Fuck this town!"

Maybe this was a sign—a sign that it was time to for us leave Hollywood? We're hicks from Canada. What were we doing here, anyway?

A few days later, it rained. Torrential downpours are rare in Hollywood, but one was happening. And this is when we learned that, not only had the robbers taken our belongings and mailbox, they'd also taken our sump pumps. Now I realize, after having to replace them, that they're well worth stealing.

Our entire laundry room flooded. All of the scripts I had written, but that hadn't "gone," came floating out. They moved past us and sailed towards the edge of our property. All the scripts that hadn't "gone," went. A sign indeed.

But in the midst of all this, we remembered the looming book party. We weren't in the mood to celebrate, but the e-vites had gone out. And come back. It was too late. People were coming, whether we wanted them to or not.

As the party approached, I tried to be in a good mood. The only way I knew how to do that was to have a few little drinks. I sipped vodka—not the celebratory champagne that we had ordered before the robbery. I supervised my housekeeper, Nadia. Her husband and ex-husband were serving as our bargain caterers.

At the party, I didn't have a good time. I was drunk, but not in that "let's all live forever" kind of way. I was drunk in that "I'm alone in a sea of people" kind of way. I wandered upstairs to our bedroom. I lay on a pile of partygoers' coats, listening to the soft sounds of the Bob Seger album I'd put on, hoping it would cheer me up. But it hadn't. The last thing I remember was the silhouette of my Pretty Wife asking me if I was okay.

I woke up later, and the house was silent. Everyone was gone. The coats had magically disappeared and my wife was sleeping beside me.

Suddenly, I felt it. The alcohol I had consumed wanted out of my body. I didn't want to wake my wife up, so I crept outside.

I peed over my neighbour's fence. (Unless you're my neighbour reading this, in which case, I peed in the washroom, washed my hands and then merely gazed over your fence.) And in this moment, I looked up at the moon. At the night sky. I was happy. I looked back at my house. My home filled with family.

Suddenly, a strong wind swept across the lip of our property, and I heard the door behind me shut.

I was now locked out of my fortified house. Surely, Pretty Wife hadn't locked *all* the doors? Yeah, after what we had just been through, she had.

I rattled some of the windows. They were latched shut. I pulled my son's foam sword from the swimming pool. Using it, I could reach upstairs to my office window. I pushed on it to see if it was open. It wasn't, but I don't think it was locked, either, so I kept lunging at it with my sword. That's when a flashlight blinded me.

"Sir?"

I turned to see a security guard.

"Sir, drop the weapon."

"No, no, no," I said. "It's not a weapon! Did I set off a silent alarm? I didn't mean to. Don't worry, it's my house."

He just glared at me.

Did I mention I wasn't wearing pyjama bottoms?

I tried to explain to the guard who I was: "I'm a comedian!"

He stared at me and spoke a burst of Spanish into his walkie-talkie.

I tried to relate. "*Yo soy* comedian."

He wasn't getting it.

"'The Daves I Know'? *Mis amigos Davido?* Do you know my housekeeper, Nadia?"

Nothing.

As the cop car arrived, two policemen jumped out. I shouted out, "I'm Bruce from *Kids in the Hall*! 'The Daves I Know'? 'My pen! My pen!'"

Nothing. I knew that I was a moment away from being tasered or shot.

Then the front door opened, and there stood my Sleepy Wife. The security guard took one look at her and gasped.

"*Ay dios mio.* You're Nancy Drew!"

I'd made a mess of the night, so I decided to sleep in my kids' room. Luckily, they were both snoring louder than I would be in a moment. I got in beside them, knowing that soon they would be too old to play "Hibernation" with me.

My Pretty Wife poked her head in.

"Is everything okay?" I asked her.

"I gave them an autograph. They were big fans of mine. It's all good."

And, as always, she had the last word.

"You know, Hollywood isn't so bad. Maybe we should stay here a little bit longer . . ."

# Acknowledgments

I used to carry my tartan notebooks to bars, play the jukebox and drink alone. But when the *Kids in the Hall* show started, people began coming up to me. "Hey Bruce . . ."

I didn't like it, because I wasn't alone anymore. See, at first, I was afraid of our fans, but over time, I've grown to love them. They made me realize I am not alone. *We* are not alone. We are all hopeful weirdos reflecting off of each other, and for this, I am thankful. So great thanks to my, and our, fans. I'd like to also thank my "boy band"—Kevin, Mark, Scott and Dave, who have made me laugh and made me better and did not murder me all those times that they should have.

I'd like to acknowledge the contribution, not just to my record collection, but to my creative life, of decades-long collaborators Brian Connelly and Craig Northey. And my first mentor, Reid Diamond.

Thanks to my collaborator and great friend, the brilliant Blake Brooker, who taught me how to get a taxi driver's life story within one minute; my "mommy," Denise Clarke; Chris "The Painter" Cran; and the tender and talented Karen Hines. Also thanks to the strong and funny Diane Flacks.

I owe great gratitude to my producer, friend and apologist, Susan Cavan, whom I'd also like to thank for allowing me to bring a crucifixion machine into the house. I'm grateful for life-long friends and fans Reverend Paul Feig and Laurie Feig. And my "EM," Janet Varney, whom I feel lucky to know and who has tirelessly supported my work. Thanks to the great Tavie for keeping the KITH torch lit all these years.

I'd like to thank David Miner and Greg Walters for steering me though the choppy waters with great love and wisdom. And show appreciation for the great tutelage of Richard Abate, Andrew Cannava, Matt Rice and Joel Begleiter. I need to thank Tammy Fox for being charming and ferocious on my behalf. And also, my smart and caring editor, Jennifer Lambert.

I would like to thank my talented right-hand woman, Amanda Sitko, who's helped me with this book and seen me in my pyjamas far too many times.

Some of the stories in this book originated in *Calgary Herald*'s *Swerve* magazine, and I think this book would not exist without their support and the enthusiasm of Shelley Youngblut.

I'd like to thank my "original" family—Ian, June, and my always sweet stepmother, Connie Buchanan—for their love and, perhaps more important, for all the material. Even more so for my hilarious, enthusiastic sister, Heather.

The dogs I've buried . . . Okay, this getting morbid.

Finally, I would like to thank my sweet and kind wife, Tracy, who threw her lot in with me with such reckless enthusiasm. And my two adorable (for now) children, who had no say in the matter.